BOA
EDITIONS
LIMITED

CONSIDERATION OF THE GUITAR

CONSIDERATION OF THE GUITAR

NEW AND SELECTED POEMS
1986–2005

by

RAY GONZALEZ

AMERICAN POETS CONTINUUM SERIES, NO. 94

BOA Editions, Ltd. ❉ Rochester, NY ❉ 2005

First Edition
05 06 07 08   7 6 5 4 3 2 1

Publications by BOA Editions, Ltd.—
a not-for-profit corporation under section 501 (c) (3)
of the United States Internal Revenue Code—
are made possible with the assistance of grants from
the Literature Program of the New York State Council on the Arts;
the Literature Program of the National Endowment for the Arts;
the Sonia Raiziss Giop Charitable Foundation; the Lannan Foundation;
the Mary S. Mulligan Charitable Trust; the County of Monroe, NY;
the Rochester Area Community Foundation;
the Elizabeth F. Cheney Foundation; the Ames-Amzalak Memorial Trust
in memory of Henry Ames, Semon Amzalak and Dan Amzalak;
the Chadwick-Loher Foundation in honor of Charles Simic and Ray Gonzalez;
the Steeple-Jack Fund; the Chesonis Family Foundation;
as well as contributions from many individuals nationwide.

See Colophon on page 208 for special individual acknowledgments.

Cover Design: Steve Smock
Cover Art: "The Unmoved" by Steve Carpenter. Courtesy of the artist.
Interior Design and Composition: Richard Foerster
Manufacturing: McNaughton & Gunn, Lithographers
BOA Logo: Mirko

Library of Congress Cataloging-in-Publication Data

Gonzalez, Ray.
   Consideration of the guitar : new and selected poems / Ray Gonzalez.— 1st ed.
      p. cm. — (American poets continuum series ; v. 94)
   ISBN 1-929918-70-4 (pbk. : alk. paper)
   I. Title. II. Series.

PS3557.O476C66 2005
811'.54—dc22

2005015358

BOA Editions, Ltd.
Thom Ward, Editor
David Oliveiri, Chair
A. Poulin, Jr., President & Founder (1938–1996)
260 East Avenue, Rochester, NY 14604
www.boaeditions.org

For my family and friends
who have supported my work over the years.

TABLE OF CONTENTS

⁎ **from *From the Restless Roots* (1986)**

Consideration of the Guitar
New Poems

SPEAK EASY

I cannot say if the sand surrounding
the horizon was there when
the first house was built.
I was not present when the birds
diminished into children walking
down a mountain road.
I would tell you if I knew how greed
becomes puzzlement and wonder
before it takes the heart into
the cottonwood shadows.

When I rejoiced at the old parrot
returning to its perch each summer,
it had been coming back for twenty years.
Why it kept appearing was written in
a book I opened at the age of five.
I read how my voice would find
the gate to the river someday,
learned to see the moment when
the blue heron folds into a piece of
paper, parchment in water that
sets the parrot free.

I cannot repeat the sun's path over
the chimneys of secret cities.
We have been there already, painting
birds with the sounds of our voices.
Is this enough to speak of perfection?
When I lead you over the trampled grasses
of yesterday, the walk you take will be
easy, birds darting over our heads
merely wings beating to the number
of centuries inside us.

THE CARVED HANDS AT SAN MIGUEL

I stood before the carved hands at San Miguel.
They could not touch the child walking home,
so they touched me.
The carved fingers were cold and hard
and they jabbed me in the heart.

When I stood back, the sculpted arms embraced
the color of the day and let me go.
When I stepped outside, I was blind.
When I tried to go back in, I was wrong.

The stone hands kept me there, promising
my sight back as soon as I knew how
to use the power of this darkness,
the need to weigh the light on the other

side against things I will never see—
the Rio Grande changing course, a hawk
throwing the sun into my mother's womb,
and the fugitive returning with gifts for
the family he abandoned in his prime.

I stood before the carved hands at San Miguel.
They could not touch me, so I held them
until I could reach beyond the wrist
and the arm—the form of rock that
became the white body left behind.

What do you approach in the rain?
Is it the scent of yesterday?
One story says you blinked when God approached.

In the other tale, you came across the border
when boundaries were trees set aflame.
Why do you hide in abandoned houses?

Are you a ghost, a fable, or a given name?
The heartbeat you follow is an instrument
played by hands that find nothing to grieve.

When you listen, you are closer to love,
which is that red canyon in the earth.
How did you fall?

One map has you lost at the river.
The page torn out of the book has you reciting an
alphabet your ancestors were too illiterate to spit.

What do you think of this?
Is it true, false,
or the comet from 1532

that split open the head of Bonifacio,
the sacrificial Lord who raised
his arms when he saw you?

Sending You

I am sending you a piece of sycamore bark.
—Paul Celan

I am sending you the shadow from
my cottonwood tree, making sure

it extends over the river to reach you.
I include the leaves in my mother's hair,

the brittle flashes of brown that
stuck to her at my birth.

I am giving you the roots from
excavated ground, their arms

reaching as far as the stone wall
where my fathers scrawled their names.

I have not forgotten the mud
from their swollen feet, rain

washing it off their labor, carrying it
beyond the storm to dry at your door.

I am delivering a cloud floating
in the sky as a memory that will

find you on the other side, passing
you flowers that grew on the earth,

their seeds the touch you needed
when you were the source of love.

I am mailing you a letter, my words you heard
when you were the sunlight that came and went,

transferring your fire into me
in the same way it burned you.

I am sending a piece of those ashes.
They spell my name as they fall into the canyon

washed out by the river, the shadow of my
cottonwood moving in the direction I came.

THE SKELETON OF THE LIZARD

The skeleton of the lizard sits on my bookshelf,
has been with me since I was a boy.

When I touch its fragile spine, it trembles in the air
like a feather about to blow away.

A piece of paper weighs more than this creature, its light
existence waiting for permission to crawl from my reach.

Every now and then, I take it out of the matchbox
where it has lived since I killed it and dried the skin.

I pull it out with tweezers as if my instrument
held someone's disbelief in the cold air.

The tiny skull of the lizard disintegrated as I grew up,
until the headless thing came at me one day,

a breeze from an open window sending it
into the room, four legs stretched like an angel,

its brittle shadow letting me catch it
in my open palm in midair.

I set it back on the shelf so it could search
for a book to hide in, tried to recall

the day, long ago, when I took its ribs
and caged a sorrow no boy can extract

from a trapped reptile, the tailbone as thin
as the white hairs that grow on my face

each time I stare at the skeleton and wait
for it to finally go away.

Every Ten Years, a Hawk Kills Before Me

Ten years ago, in my yard,
a hawk took a sparrow in
its claws and tore it apart.
I watched through binoculars
on Christmas morning,
saw the hawk pull out
the tiny heart, hold it
up to the sun in its beak,
sparrow feathers bristling
in the cold—something
I could not touch.

Last week, in autumn,
a hawk scared me by
diving near the window
to take a robin.
It glided across the street
with its catch, then dropped
the wounded bird in the grass,
its red color trying to skip away.
The huge hawk spread
its wings in the neighbor's
yard, then pounced on
tiny movement again.

The trees kept me from
seeing what happened next,
the years becoming a decade
of blood where arcs of flight
end inside each of us,
until their sharpness
is grasped every ten years
by hawks that descend
to take it away.

Runaway Train

My grandfather rode a runaway train,
left his family behind to starve
and wander the Arizona badlands.

He boarded the train without saying goodbye,
vanished like a spirit giving up the earth
for the tracks to the other side.

My grandfather flew on the runaway train as
it burned through the Superstitious Mountains,
carving new territory out of cliff walls
and the rails young men ride to die.

My grandfather escaped on a runaway train,
got out before the world war and the black
roads leveled his house and town,
wrecking his Model T Ford he used
to drive across the desert.

My grandfather slept on the moving machine,
opened his eyes when he worked the salt mines
at Yuma, digging underground in search
of air, the life promised when the engine
took him beyond the red canyons.

My grandfather took the railroad back
to my grandmother who waited at
the station, the roar of the oncoming
train telling her he would never stop,

but keep circling and signaling as
he shoveled coal, the sweat pouring
down his blackened face as
he set the locomotive on fire.

FIERCE GOD

---

after Octavio Paz

Out of the adobe
came a dark figure
singing of the morning.
It was I in another
time where I built
the walls to stay,
but they fell into
the earthquake.

Out of the passion
of the feet and hands,
I explored the suspect,
but he died of thirst.
I remained senseless
and walked under
the arches, waited
for hands to mark
the opening in the earth,

my actions forgiven
when I found
no escape,
only the smell
of goat meat
frying in the dark
and open land.

Out of the whispers
crawled a thing
searching for water,
the animal of no
shape that swallowed
my sins

and spit them back,
the glue holding
the house up
for 500 years,
the creature drinking
from the fountain,
screaming to be heard.

Out of those cries
came a fear that
took families away,
replaced the years with
rain and moratoriums,
loves and magnitudes
fit for a wiser
and negotiating man.

When I stood alone,
the shell of the house
flowered into a body
I gave up on
centuries ago,
its beautiful hair
longer than the river
threatening my kingdom
with its human gaze.

Out of that look,
months without
a soul as the walls
of mud slapped a limit
on where I could live,
what I could see and say,
how often I emerged
from the black corner
where the altar was
erected centuries ago,
the spot where my knees

fall without prayer or
the answer that must
come from me.

EMERGE

As if the sacred is the only way
and desire is fortune spilled across the desert
where no one has stepped in years.

As if the fever lifted from rage could change
the world and stir the holy water
tinged with blood.

As if the fallen song was a great mystery
and its rhyme came from the unfed mouths
of those who promised they would not weep.

As if the willow tree was a warning of green
and falling things resisting the broken ground.

As if listing the very heart of truth was outlawed
by a summer afternoon impossible to breathe.

As if each thing accomplished was taken away
by those who don't speak, but rearrange
the candles to ward off the starving spirit.

As if music in the fingers was played in time
to hear the heron rise, its flapping wings
changing the river into a pond.

As if a thousand rocks left one stone to emerge
through the decaying monument where no
one said anything as the mountain arrived.

As if the one thing we believe was finally
played on a guitar carved from the wood
of our father's crib.

As if the darkness is the beloved teacher
and its tool the mightiest reason
to go there together, unafraid.

As if the sacred is the only way
and the difficulties are lined up on the shelf
decorating the hallway into the interior

where the names we are called
are the names of those who emerge.

Into

Into the desert in search of signatures.
Into the cage to retrieve the laughing man.

Into the hair to trace the blood vein.
Into the sky to follow the bird.

Into the language to congregate everything.
Into the moisture to recall the love.

Into the fish to see the lion.
Into the snake to calm the father.

Into the orange to peel the lemon.
Into the apple to destroy the seed.

Into the garden to stand up again.
Into the name to drown the past.

Into the swollen ground to scare up a new forest.
Into the body to forgive the sparrow.

Into the border wire to sweat alone.
Into the mountain shadow to bear the light.

Into the question to argue about the dragonfly.
Into the smile to amplify the scream.

Into the pattern to kneel alone.
Into the scarf without a face.

Into the sleep to choose the rain or the moon.
Into the morning to eat at the table.

Into the house to ignore one room.
Into the room to parachute toward earth.

Into the brain to stay alive.
Into the sound to adore the music.

Into the belly button as the flaming wheel.
Into the eyes so no words will appear.

Into the palm to feel what is hidden.
Into the truth to massage its wings.

STOPPING ALONG THE RIO GRANDE NORTH OF HATCH, NEW MEXICO

No one speaks to the water or
sees the flowing lines as they pass
and become the path to the end.
The depths have fallen while
cottonwoods and salt cedars rise
at the great bend,
the curve where I flee their
proclamation without wanting
the mineral rites of the last
person who died here.

No one has entered the water
since the year of the yellow mist
or helped a loved one come across.
When the swift current was eternity,
the first man waited on a lonely
spot no one else had seen.

I would not think of this,
could not stand here and wait for
the gentle sleep of lifetimes ago
when this river broke toward
a landing on its bank,
submerged logs secret devotions
to what I can't give as I slip
in the mud and almost fall in,
sand cranes lifting above yellow reeds,
their wings the maps lost without
knowing the difference between
nostalgia and my words carried
off by soaring shadows.

THE LIGHT AT MESILLA

It was a broken treaty woven
into past streets of dust,
not great belief, but a way
to get there before a line of music
glistened on the walls.
It could not be the illusion of horses
streaming against the river.
The river was gone.
The water was God taking back
the earth, wrapping the mountains
with a surface of faith, a point of
light unknown to the dirt in the eye.
It was the blowing of clay on the lips,
the jars filled with secret drink
that would not steam or fill
hidden basements with fumes,
those rooms already black
with corn and *ristras* of chiles
turning to stone.

The light touched the altar
in the alley, gave it treasures of ice
that invented prayer, burned
words upon the mouths
of those who knelt there,
ignoring the breaking radiance
as they fled into the plaza
where the fire had been.
It was not a sacrifice
allowed in the days
of illumination,
nights when it stunned
the cold person standing
under the bright arches.

It was a saying—
"Look at the light" where
the adobe is cracked,
turning to fine powder
that hid what came before,
dropping to the ground
as tiny wicks of candles
no one would ignite.

ASCENDING THE STONE STEPS AT THE GRAN QUIVIRA RUINS

The pain in my legs increases
as I climb, wondering if the trees
below will wait for me.
Grabbing handholds in the rock,
I take the stone steps up,
this height traveling with me
to touch the ancient signs.

Here is the level where the blue jay
stopped, there the flash of white
where I once saw a pair of hands
mounted as bone against rock.
I move in the cold and a crow calls
without knowing where I am,
vertigo dancing as I look down
in time to spot a trail of smoke in
the sky that waited years for me.

I keep going up, the narrow path
worn down into a dream where
few men ever return, the promises
of elevation mysteries in their tired
hearts, their resting hole at the crest
the only fire I will never see.

I climb steps to leave the wilderness
behind, a hollow chamber greeting me
when I stop. Black walls, no blood.
I am greeted by the shattered tree where
someone fired an arrow into the bark.
Here is the resin on my hands from
the superstition that to feel these

boulders is to find the body
that lives at the top.

I totter there and wait,
mountains to the north and south
threatening each other with
the black reach of a short day
when the valley below does
not catch up with the truth,
ignoring the impassible ceiling
of time I can't reach, the ledges
above holding the place
where many died, some rose,
a few giving birth to the turning
tide that took the people away.

Breathing easy, breathing hard,
I turn to the west where the sun falls
before I can name the voices
that taught me young:
San Lorenzo, Chimayo, shadows
at Aguirre Springs that fell
into the cliffs the way
the crow returns,
its flight marking my path
before the stone steps vanish
and I see I will make it down.

ANDRÉ BRETON AT ZUNI PUEBLO, 1945

The snakes are in his eyes
as he searches for *Hawikuh*,
mirror of stones he dreamed of in Paris.
His breathing is harder, fire entering his belly
as he staggers between painted walls
to find his umbilical cord preserved
in a clay jar on the dirt floor.
When the silent Zuni man points to it,
Breton opens the lid, his escaping birth
exploding in his eyes, the dead coyote
in the arroyo jumping off the ground
to run into the hills.

Breton wants to speak, say
the poem that made his feet sore,
swollen legs trembling in the dirt
because he is finally in the kiva—
the hole in his head he has reamed
with his tongue over and over.
As he stares into his birth in the jar,
sweat on his forehead runs green and blue,
wavering thoughts skipping over the ruins
until he spots a piece of turquoise
embedded in the rock.

He lifts the stone and looks behind him.
The pointing man is gone, but two other
Zuni with no heads stand there, arms crossed,
holes in their chests steaming an orange mist
Breton has seen before.
He drops the rock.
The turquoise stays in his palm.
As he turns to hand it to the headless men,
they run, the orange mist forming

a trail in the air behind them,
its fine cloud surrounding Breton
as he staggers toward the cliffs to meet
each secret thing he has ever done.

Rattlesnakes Hammered on the Wall

Seven of them pinned in blood by
long, shiny tails, three of them still

alive and writhing against the wood,
their heaviness whipping the wall

as they try to break free,
rattles beating in unison,

hisses slowly dying in silence,
the other four hanging stiff

like ropes to another life,
patterns of torn skin dripping

with power and loss, the wonder
of who might have done this

turning to shock as all seven
suddenly come alive when

I get closer, pink mouths
trembling with white fangs,

lunging at me then falling back,
entangled in one another to form

twisted letters that spell a bloody
word I can't understand.

In the Time of the Totem

after Max Ernst's sculpture Capricorn

When you peer from under
the totem, you are mistaken for
the returning son who carved
the pole with bleeding knuckles,
assumed the sun would split in two
and give you more light.
Have you counted the wooden
faces atop one another?
When you miss the one
that fell off the pole,
he will go farther than
your greatest art, returning
as a spear decorated with symbols
your ancestors misspelled.
Have you overlooked
the horns on his head
and listened to the woman
who loves you?
When you make love to her
in the red mud,
seeping layers will fill her with
your first child, forcing you
to read the ancient book your father
hid inside the hollow head at
the top of the highest totem
you have climbed.

THE WOLF TABLE

What started as rain became the eye lost in heaven.
Upon the green shadow, the snowflake that forgot
winter was yesterday, the answer to the dandelion riddle,
the tongue bitten accidentally, hurting the mouth
before finding space to change the books.
To stay against what is no longer there,
belief woven into the rock. Smooth nights
equal one bending of the knee. To find
the summer solstice is afraid and it is easy
to pretend the stars were psalms
that have not been read.

Only a miracle could bring back the empty plate,
a perfect apple and the clay mask disintegrating
into the face of the father on the wall.
Yet, the siren is a thousand miles away,
blessing someone else's youth.
Structure counterflames the tongue
and allows the wolf under the table
to lap moisture from tired feet.
A scene with house and pasture,
the mouse between the lapped toes
and a bee inside the stomach,
a horse in the field and the ants
in the shoes with the wolf between the teeth.

Choice of web, spider or eye
weaving into meticulous scent,
the everlasting thread to the ceiling
where droplets gleam in response,
torn engines thriving for air, masking
the streets with glass cut to ward off
the knives and fists, the dance following
the animal's path under atomic arches,

inside acoustic trios that sit on chairs
of concrete and play what was harvested
when the trains took over and lettuce yards
covered the shells that never exploded,
alcoholic gunners too busy igniting
their liquor on a Catholic priest.

The garden of this shame in the armpit
of the statue embedded during
the childhood of a forgotten genius
who would paint the wolf someday.
When the world ends, the garden of shame
will grow two trees—a small yellow thing
that bristles with tears, the second a willow
from the undiscovered river behind the brain.

When the genius falls in love for the first time,
the black Madonna of his dreams will enter
the country to ward off pleasure, giving him
a child who shall never plant gardens, but go
live under the yellow tree, ignoring
the willow until its branches grow higher
and his insect instructors swarm to teach him,
keeping him ahead of the beetle that lands
on his shoulders, then flies out of the way
of the wolf under the table that searches for
the man who will not be named for his father,
but wind up holding an unshaved
flower to give to his mother instead.

Immediacy

Love in this age of screens and crosses,
  broken saxophones winding down
the stairs to set fire to the skirts of girls.

Love in the capsized corridors of perfume
  where distant fathers sleep on the walls,
their century old beards growing beyond

decoration, the gallery of fine dust bringing
  their sons to stare and stare.
Love in the idea of cascading waterfalls,

blue fish flying up the curtains to obtain sorrow,
  spawn erasures of memory inside water
where love invented the idea of evolution.

Love in the piano keys of divorce, the whispers
  lasting a lifetime, making the couple order more wine,
shadows at their table moving closer to what

might have been, glasses tinkling, smoke
  arriving, the story of a crafted wildness
lost before an expensive meal.

Love in the year of taking, then asking,
  love promoted as extinct starfish,
their patterns on the foreheads of the forgiven

slowly turning red as the night deepens,
  as those lovers touch what they
weren't suppose to find, the starfish

dreaming it is only love and there is
  a blue current hurtling them
to a deeper cave on the other side.

The Hiding

Who are you to tell me the frog
was orange and gave you blue fire?

When I saw my own, it was a toad
and its color was not in the books.

There is hope in the cringing leaves.
What I hide under there is more
valuable than my shoes.

The house of my childhood still stands.
I went there once and knocked.

No one answered.
How can you say it was the wrong
town in another country?

Everything has to sleep and choose.
Each moment yearns to be the first.

It is a scar I touch when I travel,
my hairline as invisible
as the first son being born.

Everything I tell you is a secret.
Do not remove the pelican pendant
from your neck.

There is nothing in the lake where
the blue heron lifted and disappeared.

What if I lie awake all night
in search of its shape?

What if I tell you I saw
a woman talking to herself?

She had my mother's voice
and my father's dreams.

Everything waits for this to be.
Each leaf I hid in my hands
I found later in your wild hair.

He reached for the stars
and found the galaxy
of his mother's milk,
waited for the sucking fire
to turn into a hunger
he could chart
among her cries.

He asked for the heavens
and met the limestone walls
instead, glowed in the canyons
like a lost comet rearranging
the story of the planet.

He reached for the stars
and raged at the darkness
outshining the light,
dismissed the abandoned
continent of his birth

as the landscape of his
father's enormous forehead,
the wrinkled skin sweating
as the old man reached down
and took his wife again.

THE HORNS AT SIERRA LADRONE, NEW MEXICO

after Robert Wrigley

I focus on the ocotillo branch,
wasps dancing through the brittle hair of straw,
missing the spider webs stretched across the path.
I avoid the thorns, watch two owls depart in flight,
red ants streaming on the ground.
Someone hides on the other side of
the stream whose bells ring like water
tracing the earth too late.
He has followed my trail,

folds of green leaves and cactus bulbs
steering us to imperfection as we see
what we have been told:
There are elk horns up in a tree.
We were asked to bring them back,
take the scars out of the tree in the season
that kills the rain, the horns becoming
local legend before they disappear.

They are entangled a few feet above
the ground in the branches of the pine,
perhaps there for years, the elk shedding
its horns the way I avoid the cave beyond.
The rocks in the opening are lined
with moss, a place I have known.
Staring at the cave, I have been inside before,
blind and afraid of movement that pulled at
the mighty head and took the horns.
I won't emerge from there, climb to
the sun instead, the cliff a forgiven thing
as I hear the rattler nearby.
I can't see it, stick my thumb in a prickly
pear instead, meet the challenge of the matted grass,

the quick blue jay, the pause of
the man stalking himself below.
I think fire, but cannot kiss the skin,
a sudden rodent disappearing
under a rotting trunk.

As I step again, a rumble in the distance.
When I turn to find the dark clouds,
the one who was hiding stands and runs.
In his footprints, I see the way down.
In his serving ground, he leaves a sign for me.
In his carvings on the tree, perhaps my name.
I go back to the horns, want to pull them
from the branches, but can't reach them

or touch the fading white of those
twisted swords that were left for me.
The thunder nears as I slip on the slick floor
of leaves, go down easy to sit against the tree,
under the horns that point to the far road.
When I get to my knees, I hear the breaking
and splintering, a shadow bringing the story
I've wanted about the man who ran out of here.

A Poem in Every Direction

The first line written on September 10th, 2001, the night before the attack on the World Trade Center in New York.

The world is going to explode.
The world is going to miss itself.
Won't you celebrate the secret in its hands?
Won't you rename the alphabet to spell your wish?

I have preserved the leaf under my shoe,
given it a name and returned it to the earth.
This is desire for the cure,
the first imprint of what survived.
There is no life in the 24 hours of the wheel.

It is a beautiful day when the distance falls.
Would you please read the rest of the sky?
The wind believes what you say.
The earth renames itself with the present past.
Won't you kiss the willow tree when it grows,
lie down between bodies that have forgiven you?
I have sent the sound to the nearest sea,
moved out of the way and waited for
instructions from our nourished greed.

The world writes on one piece of paper,
the globe shining like missiles never fired.
How can you diminish their light without
explaining your bloody feet?
In memory, God told me the winter came.
In one idea, I honored the puzzle as the life of art.
In memory, God punished the keepers of dead fish.
In one idea, I swallowed the canning jars.
In memory, God said the towel is for the sweat of the King.
In one idea, I turned in every direction and prayed.

This is how the stage lights up,
gathers the might of the sparrow and turns it
into the love for concrete.
May we swallow the dust of air, spin into
cocoons stronger than our hands.

The world is counting its shoes again,
the globe a sermon set on fire by the Milky Way.
This is a statement for silence,
a sentence for the white page.

It is past present when the metropolitan camps are filled.
Look, the apples are bleeding on the trees.
It is gentleness when fortunes are lost.
Kind folk have turned the crowded corner.
Someone is going to love the idea of knowing this.

In dancing, God sweated and drank bottled water.
In one life, I was afraid and lay down.
In dancing, God ate his fast food and ordered more.
In one life, I was a dragonfly pinned to a strip of wood,
loved my blue wings when motion was a map
and I was stuck there without speech.
In dancing, God tore telephone messages to shreds.
I called again, but the orchestra had put its instruments away.
The world is going to smoke.
I am filling the language with sticks.
The world will be renamed the earth.
I quit searching for the Aztec calendars centuries ago.
The world is going to listen.
I wish I could hear the sleeping crickets.
The world is watching on untouchable screens.
I am folding origami into failed patterns.
The world is going to be the earth
as I take those folds and turn them
into blossoms I have never seen.

FEVER

We train for the cold
and dream we are alive,
know no one,
but are loved by all.

When we take off our clothes,
the medals cling to the heart,
but we don't feel them
and go on living.

Inside the arena, two young boys
wait for the signal, hushed crowds
sweating under the lights before
waking on a burned street.

When we hold hands,
we move down the alley,
point to the corner where
we saw our fathers go down.

There is no end to this.
Scars on our faces twitch with love,
other expressions crossing
the street and never coming back.

Inside the arena, one strong man is left.
The crowd cheers and demands
the blood given upon admission
will be the blood taken home.
Hours under the lights and the hidden
jars of beer. When the crowd
steps into the night, marked cars
are waiting and every gun is a surprise.

CONSIDERATION OF THE GUITAR

To pause huge and forgiven without
haunches taken inside the rattle
votive lips torn between sadness
staring at flipped cages exploding cinders
illegal survivors demanding implications

To stop the bathtub from becoming the guitar
stains on windows feeding eyesight
spreading reliance catching Maturca
strumming woman of thumbprint recognition
illegal eyelids overwhelmed by traffic tickets

fingering chords to survive bare backs
jurisdiction factory border dweller lifting
plastic globes giving them eyes to watch
Mexican guitars melt into instruments
assured upon outlawed entry

To clean the spine of ambition
spying on the bone the problem
before acoustic evacuation scripture
comic books from electric Halotinga predator
guitar pick knife pointing to barbed wire

buried on border railroad tracks humming
with sincerity when songs end rubber sandals
worn by a guitarist text unread pictographs carried
by domestic maids cleaning brains from oven corridors
freed from amplified rebellion descendents of democracy

To shoot the crossing pass the news
volcanic boulevards rally beaten barrios moving
the unachieved bottleneck screaming until
they listen take their figs beat their children
ten thousands years of damaged guitar lessons

To stop what could have been summoned
Logolista of blazing feedback Spanish
the lizard's eye happening again splitting
Hendrix faces on seams of border patrol bodies
decomposing harmonies to cross the river

To know the husband leaks in another language
knowledge as amplified *tinctura* wind basket damage
lighting secret police vans hiding what happened
giving heat climate the guitar stage guns
unaware a salad of feet approaches every night

To let approach take place
decide the fence holds illegals without asking
who went first who gave in last who allowed
Tlachelolo to rise out of bent labor elbows
and hit the lead notes again and again

To tear words placed in stone
release beans to feed pickled hearts left behind
as the captured flee before the river floods
rooftops where myths don't lie guitars
boiling water to electrocute the other side

This desert fleeing metals damaged bridges
interrogation pens counted boys breaking strings
Madres taking their time blessing themselves
Geronimo's death mask painted white to resemble
the flat-nosed rattler that pulled the plug

To pause before the final song
see the lungs as key embrace
hairpins finding beauty in border crescendo
not one illegal fugitive saying a word
unplugged diamonds embedded in their temples

government switches flipped
triggers timed to explode as the faces
in the barbed wire dust open their eyes
to stare at the wall of amplifiers
and guitar windows play on

The Walls

Julius Caesar's head was cut off
and fed to the barbarians waiting
outside the walls of Rome.
Salvador Dali wore one orange
sock and a white one on days
he went to eat breakfast in cafes.
On days he stared at the wall,
he did not wear socks.

Yukio Mishima sheathed his knives
in walls of whale oil, claiming such
creatures were the only ones that
understood the art of sacrifice.
The last thing John Lennon saw
before he was gunned down was
the brick wall of his apartment house.

Sitting Bull had fourteen wives
he lined up against the cliff walls.
He would close his eyes and walk
blindly to them with an erection,
promising he would take the first
one his erection touched.
Crazy Horse watched silently
from the cliff walls above.

J. D. Salinger scribbled on his bedroom
walls as a boy, promising his mother
to whitewash the figures the first
time he was caught.
Joan of Arc climbed over the walls
and fell on top of a castle guard,
the commotion bringing soldiers
who swore the wall opened and
she escaped by stepping through.

Nikita Khrushchev stared at the wall
of nuclear buttons and knew
it was a green one they told him to push,
but the triggers were every color except green.
Hernán Cortés' men met a wall
of arrows, then turned and ran.
Montezuma's men met a wall of armor,
wept, then stoned their chief off the wall
for helping the conquistadores.

Carl Jung opened his eyes to find himself
sleeping against a wall of flowers,
the beautiful smell giving him the answer
he had been looking for.
Charlie Chaplin ordered his crew to remove
the hidden mirror from the wall, footage
of his latest lover overflowing
onto the studio floor.

Sor Juana de la Cruz hid her new poem
in a hole in the wall, but when a fellow nun
went to retrieve it after Sor Juana's death,
it was gone.
The Dalai Lama stopped in the snow
and bowed his head to pray before the wall
of dead monks killed by the Chinese.

Virginia Woolf's last memory before drowning
was the wall of family portraits, the photographs
of her father and brothers so radiant in the river fog.
Billy the Kid simply dug a hole in the adobe wall
of the jail with his bare hands and walked away.

Janis Joplin was found dead of an overdose
in her Los Angeles hotel, her face facing the wall.
Federico García Lorca did not face any walls
when he was shot under the trees.

No one knows how Tu Fu encased himself
in a wall of bamboo, staying inside the tube
for ten years, never saying a word, his feet
becoming the roots of bamboo within
the first few months of his silence.
Al Capone stared at the walls of his cell
in Alcatraz and added the bank figures again,
trying to get them right.

Babe Ruth heard a thud against the wall
of his hotel suite, the baseball rolling down
the hallway as a signal his tryst with the team
owner's wife was about to be revealed.
William Shakespeare stared at the empty walls
of the theatre, stood there without saying
a word, and stared at the empty walls of the theatre.

Geronimo extended his arms over the walls
of rock, the approaching sound of the cavalry
troops echoing down the canyon, the pictograph
Geronimo carved high on the wall, years ago,
lifting him to safety.
Two days before Salvador Allende was assassinated,
Pablo Neruda, dying of cancer, woke at Isla Negra
to find the walls of the room where he lay
were covered in hundreds of clinging starfish.

THE BURNING

The Burning Moon

The burning moon gives away its spirit.
When I look up to catch it, the yellow
fields borrow my tongue.

The Burning Chair

The burning chair is carved from hope,
smells of patient wood and flames
toward the last person it held.
The chair loves its emptiness, ignites
when the city is saved by a flood
of smoking people.

The burning chair stands on the black
floor as the spot no one wants
to claim they have sat in.

The Burning Monkey

The burning monkey teaches me.
He feeds me fire from things he knows.
The monkey is brave, climbs buildings
and grabs airplanes.

When I let him go, he escapes to the jungle
where there are pyramids being climbed
by men chased by burning apes.

The Burning Eye

The burning eye yields a vision,
holds the key to blue starlight
before the ovens of history
are removed by skeleton-thin men.

The eye stares into the canyon of shouts,
sees the fire and looks down at its bare chest
and its tattoos, blinks when a plume of smoke
carries a message sizzling in its smoldering pupil.

The Burning Tortilla

The burning tortilla fattens the wind,
lights the kitchen with smoke from quiet meals,
blue stoves and the masa of a tired house.

The tortilla disintegrates into black
fingertips where the roads are alleys
and the empty table is not a dream.

The Burning Trumpet

The burning trumpet is child to the lips,
its blower sweating in the spotlight.
The trumpet spins on the needle, vinyl days
turning, cries of the dark man the notes
broken by the flames of time.

The trumpet is branding the lips,
its player weaving off stage.
The trumpet vibrates on a silver dollar,
the shoes of the composer sitting freshly shined
next to his empty carrying case.

The Burning Mouth

The burning mouth kisses everything,
doesn't tire of smooching the body
of the last one hundred years.

The mouth blows O smoke rings
with its perfect lips, embers of desire
lighting the way for the breast hanging
in the fog of possession.

The Burning Grasshopper

The burning grasshopper alighted
on my shoulder. I turned and it
sizzled in surprise.
When the summer came,
I tried to be happy.

When the grasshopper fried,
it made me wise.
The thing ate my wishes.
When it was full, it fell at my feet,
the grasshopper smoking
in the wind of my cherished dream.

The Burning River

The burning river has no course.
Its chemicals cross borders aligning the future.
The water changes direction when
green fires float upon it.

The river knows gravity, goes south
to leave black clouds over territories.
When the river finally explodes, it will
be an ocean with maps of new countries,
fresh ways of setting water on fire.

The Burning Tomb

The burning tomb holds the teeth
of my old father.
The tomb encloses the keys to his last
burned-out car.
The tomb lies before an altar of ashes.

The tomb is buried on the other side
of the desert, its walls rising to be studied
by centuries of burning men.

The Burning Spider

The burning spider bit me.
When I grabbed it between two fingers,
it made a crisp sound and went out.

The spider was reborn.
When I smelled my fingers,
it was the scent of leaving.

The Burning Hand

The burning hand placed itself over my heart.
When it got there, I was safe.
When it touched me, I did not burn.
The hand abandoned my town,
covered my family with ashes.
When I went there, the petrified bodies were
beautiful and some of them reached for me
with outstretched hands.

MEMORIZE

Memorize the ashes from the last century.
Brush the wind off your hair.

The language of startled equality brings you
words from the broken dish and the singing scarf.

Sometimes you walk afraid.
Other times, there are moths fluttering in the shadows.

The eye is passion and no one forgets.
You will wake without a drop of water

and take the same road where your friend slept
and the door of recollection deceived the thinker

and the son, even the one who loved you.
When time runs out, the listeners understand.

Plan yourself by counting the angels twice,
laughing at how your faith was taken by

the swollen river where the current flowed
and bits of resurrection were thrown at your feet.

Your first chance was a fragrance that spelled the future.
Your second was the silence after salutation.

The secret is to keep the fireflies at your back.
They will demand darkness as a goodbye kiss.

Call them light.
Call them what never happened and never will.

What emerges determines where you live,
how you trace the dirt in your hands as

the remains you dreamed about
without surrendering to the silly dream.

If this is muttered in your throat, you will forget.
If it is too late for the clay bowl, someone suffered in your place.

Some of your legends remain for no reason,
extracted from books too luminous to read.

Memorize their startling answers.
Take them with you and cross the river

where a different story was told.
Be sad and wiser than the tumbleweed.

Your mouth will turn into a staircase falling
toward your house where the grass gains,

the tree lives, and the parchment closes in.
After the closing, think of this:

There are thoughts inside the wrinkled leaf,
under the lost shoe and on the fossil

you found the day you returned
without involving the world.

I Have Been Served

I have been served by the black widow
hiding behind the swamp cooler, its black
marble crawling across the wood to
return me to my childhood, been served
by the old man selling snow cones in
the heat, his hat falling over his eyes
to ward off boys who want his melting ice.

I have been given by the blue lizard
trembling on the fence before vanishing
with its tail left wriggling in my hand,
been delivered by the desert wind,
brown clouds hiding the roads,
exposing the arms of the mountains
as a place to go hide.

I have been near the adobe walls
cracking in the village, startled by
their way of turning black in
the night and disappearing,
been served by the lost
children in the dirt streets,
their hands full of pennies
reaching out to me for more.

I have been filled by the white
crosses in the cemeteries,
the names of my ancestors
fading from stone memory,
been drenched by the river
as border, its water breaking
countries into two sides,

been directed by the highway
fleeing west to the burning
horizon where the sun waits for
no one to arrive, been served by
the silence of going back to 1954
without the fear of smelling
the tortillas my grandmother
left burning on the stove.

THE PROMISES OF GLASS

Do not look. It is still the earth.
Things have been carried out of
the libraries to make you a passenger.

When the dead man gave bread to the circus,
he was applauded. When the ballot boxes
were absent of ideas, the country changed.

Do not worry. It is still your home.
It pays to keep a family album to show strangers
how you were given private rooms where

you traced deep currents and collections of glass—
old bottles, cups from festivals where winners
were dogs, rich couples as givers of patterned bowls.

Do not close your eyes. It is the hour
you promised by not speaking to anyone
for months, simply polished your glass

to share what you gained—a forest or two,
frightening mountains where concerts for paradise
are played, all this after years of rubbing glass,

your fingers as smooth as the surfaces of tomorrow
you search for as you wipe the dust off
rows of bottles you never knew you had.

Hymn for the Tongue

There is nothing more to say.
Chile pods in the nose and on the tongue.

When the fire strikes, raise your hand to be
recognized as a new element in the universe

long after everyone has disappeared.
Light can't be mentioned here,

only the girl on the street who warned you
you had to translate desire into a flowery thing

after killing fourteen scorpions
at your mother's house in one week,

the awful things springing from the walls
day and night, making you fear your appetite,

the hooked tails you gathered in a sandwich bag
causing a commotion across the stars,

galaxies imploding to get out of your way when
you touched the largest stinger with a fingertip,

sent the cosmos flying to find ways to feed itself,
means of being able to speak with you.

THE MASK

What have you saved?
What have you given up
so there can be dust
in the clarity of things?
When the soundless dancer
is the first thing you see
in the morning,
something has changed.
You are no longer frightened
by unexplainable grief.

There is an endless moon
in the sky but you gave it
a different name.
What have you saved?
What passes for a voice
in the magnified moment
of crying the way
the cricket sings?
The iron mask on your wall
is missed by the mummy
shrouded in earth.
When you helped others
dig it up, the air was cold
for an instant, but it was
something you could believe.

How sharp should the color
of a knife be?
When you handle it,
the story you carve
in the tree has already
been told, your late arrival
expected after bits

of the night came
apart in your hands.
What have you kept?
How have you lived?

ANOTHER

after Li-Young Lee

Another word for understanding is *light*,
as in the light that leaves the mind
and kneels over the garden.
Another pause is the time the sun takes
to illuminate the truth:
No one has arrived.
Magnolia, rhododendron, daisies
that line the path.

Another word for knowing is *darkness*,
as in the falling bird that lands
in the green and disappears.
To stand here is to tear memory,
its given wind floating a piece of paper
that clings to the screen door:
Oblivion, mercy, the language of
those who lost the note.

Another word for caught is *see*,
as in "See the circle take shape.
Look at how the other side
was lost, unable to join hands
with what we were giving away."

The last word for stealth is *purity*,
as in the easy form of our faces
reaching out to become the rain,
opening our eyes to the silver raven,
the knowing basket, the idea we
are being given a chance to stay.

After Reading Rexroth, I Stand by the Rio Grande

Look at how we start over, hypnotized by
the mountains falling into the river.

See how many brown men have crossed,
their hands tied behind their backs, their wives

and children disappearing in the scent of mimosa
and salt cedar hanging over the water.

Bring those trees to their farthest height.
Bring your shoes to the edge of the mud.

When they pull some bodies out,
the hawk soars.

When they count the numbers,
food on the plate grows cold.

Look at how we start over, so far
from the soul of the current.

Look at the defeated snake, the sinking worm,
that ocotillo bush bristling with thorns

once worn around the neck
of the invisible Lord.

Tied behind his back was the knotted cross,
the unfaithful scar, the Spanish mark

that cut this river into
pieces of worn gold.

Breathe the humid body and let go.
Breath the cottonseed in the air, then cough.

When you go back to tree one,
break off a branch.

At tree two, hang a strand of your hair.
When the third tree blocks your path, you are there.

CELEBRATE

I am going to carry my river to the end
of the earth and celebrate.
I am going to wear my hat, then
whisper to the mice under the floor,
not hesitate in asking the stars to quit
burning so I can teach myself my
own prayers for a change.

When the car comes for me,
I will get in and be taken away.
The road will be full of birds,
sparrows and cardinals that flew
away from me long ago.
When I reach the moon,
my father will already be there,
wearing his own hat.
He will send me back on
the same river, my beard longer
than the white hair on the head
of the angriest god.

I will set foot on the driest land, wait
for the trees to grow and teach me
how to live under their shade.
I am going to love the places
where I have never been,
emerge from under those trees
in time to greet the stranger
who says to me, "Late. Late.
You are very late."

MY BROTHERS

My brothers lie under the darkened stones.
When I wake them, they ask my name.
When I answer, they disappear
and I keep polishing the stones.

My brothers sleep under the stones.
When I interpret their dreams,
the cracks in the ground grow flowers
and I am no longer alone.

My brothers travel under the rocks.
When they pass under my feet,
I move out of the way and they pause,
wait for me to take the wrong step.

My brothers tell stories under the rubble.
When I am left out of the legend, tree roots
grow to the horizon, their underground
roads never crossing my path.

My brothers hold hands under the stones.
When they grip tighter, the world wants to end.
When they let go, I run to stand under
a huge cottonwood in an open field.

My brothers are missing under the rocks.
When I build a house where I last saw them,
no one wants to visit because there are
always voices coming out of the walls.

My brothers are tired of being mistaken for stones.
When I throw another armful in the pile,
their widows take years to select one pebble
in their hands before walking away.

My brothers seek justice under the stones.
When I start digging with a shovel,
they shift their skeletal bones to trick me
into thinking I have dug out their hearts.

My brothers rattle the space under the rocks.
Their history will be uncovered someday,
but there are too many rivers that
flow without a name.

My brothers lie under the darkened stones.
When they tell me to join them,
I say I am finally coming and a new
continent rises out of the earth.

from
The Hawk Temple at Tierra Grande
2002

THERE WILL BE CENTURIES

after Thylias Moss

Pianos will be moved from house to house,
giant machines trembling at the hands of the composer.

Men will climb out of white cars
in parking lots where miracles have happened.

Tiny lizards will cling to the chests of boys,
so they aren't captured by cold hands and killed.

Goats will be slaughtered by drunken uncles tired of
burning their tongues on the naked backs of their mistresses.

Spaceships will hover in the dreams of children taken
by their parents to be shown where the light comes from.

Riddles will be shipwrecked
on the pure enamel of a fingernail.

The owl will fly as a prisoner of its own silence,
teaching us how the hole in the saguaro

is the center of a darkness
the new century cannot claim.

Computer viruses will become actual beetles,
soft wires turning to green and blue lines populating

the house the lovers abandoned, transparent wings
buzzing the air of the woman as she flees,

insect armies giving the man time to dress
before they surround him with sound.

The white iguana will be captured in the photo
of the year 2000, where those who love

these things give up wanting to see them,
surrendering to the inflated chest of the lizard,

its red bubble ballooning to the size of a spirit
the illegal alien claimed when he entered the country.

There will be quiet weeping, what I am saying
mistaken for a postcard left on a table.

Lalo Jimenez will join Juan Sanchez as the explorers
found alive in the river, their notes mentioning

the two-head salamander without one word
about what was cut out of their hearts,

the puma that consumed their mothers,
the claws collected by their fathers,

their grandmothers and Cabeza de Baca walking
out of a desert named Chihuahua.

Tiny Clay Doll with No Arms

Given to me by my sister as a gift,
the tiny Indian doll stands with no arms.

Received so I can raise my hands
and stop the world from getting closer.

Something has been taken from here—
a day when reaching out was death.

Something has been lost
with my own hands.

The doll stands three inches tall,
its brown head wrapped in a red scarf.

No arms, as if I could look at a body
and not welcome it back.

As if I knew what happened
to my grip on things.

The clay doll stands on my bookshelf.
It stares out the window.

It does not have any arms.
I don't know why it was carved that way,

don't know what it means, why
invisible palms hold everything together.

When I touch the doll with a fingertip,
it leans against a book.

It does not fall.
When I set it back on

its bare feet, I carefully use
both of my sweating hands.

For those who ran in the streets,
there were no faces to welcome them back.
José escaped and loved the war.

For those who swam with bitterness
of a scorched love,
there was a rusted car to work on.

For those who merely passed
and reclined in prayer,
there was the tower and the cross.

For those who dedicated tongues
to the living and dying,
there were turquoise painted doorways.

For those who left their children
tied to the water heater,
there was a shout and a name.

For those whose world
was real and beautiful,
there was a cigarette and a saint.

For those who asked José
to stay and feed his children,
there were flowers at their funerals.

For those who carried a shovel
tattooed on their backs,
there was a wet towel and a bottle.

For those who swept the street
of superstition and lie,
there was the house to come home to.

For those who came home late
and put their swollen feet up,
there was love and the smell of dirty socks.

For those who feared the devil
and spit on his painted arms,
there was a lesson in rosaries.

For those who had to leave
before the sun went down,
there was asphalt and a bus.

For those who stared at wet plaster
and claimed the face of Christ appeared,
there was confinement and stale bread.

For those who talked with each other
and said it was time to go,
there was lead in the paint and on the tongue.

For those who left children behind,
there was a strange world
of sulphur and sparrow nests.

For those who accused their ancestors
of eating salt, there were these hands
tracing what was left after the sweat.

I HEAR THE BELLS OF THE ICE CREAM VENDOR OUTSIDE MY DOOR

The sign on his cart says Pancho's Ice Cream.
Pifas, my cousin, beats me to the *raspa* treats,

the ice cream vendor pushing his cart as I cross the bridge.
The wind knocks me over, lifts me near the cliffs.

A thousand feet below, purple rocks take me
farther away from my early streets.

The sign appears again—Pancho's Ice Cream.
I hear the bells and his cries, "*Paletas! Paletas!*"

The man pushes his cart, leaves me hanging
off the bridge, a tornado striking my mother's house,

ice from snow cones flying across the chasm of fear
as I reach the other side of the bridge.

I wake in the trees of a flavor I never tasted,
my lost cousin dead in Vietnam, bells of the vendor

ringing in my ears as I buy two snow cones—
one for Pifas and one for me. I eat mine

in darkness as the second drips
strawberry red in my cold hands.

KIVA FLOOR AT ABO

What do I know in my confusion?
How does it shape my legs and arms
as they sink deeper into the earth,
ancient red walls smothering something
I was taught long ago, forgotten words
written in a place I will never look?
If I hear the drum, I am mistaken.
To ask for directions is to pretend
I can identify three or four worlds
where no pumas were trapped
to strengthen this room.

It is the whispering that taught me
how the white dot in the window
is larger than itself—
its dimensions injuring several families
before healing them of ambition.
What if I can't climb out and dirt
warnings explode over my arms?
Skin inside second skin where
the afternoon reveals how far
the wooden ladder goes down.
To descend is to listen.

Climbing back up kills necessity,
shards littering the floor in patterns
I saw when my troubles began.
Though I speak softly, the galaxy
embedded in these old bricks
will not emerge, the search
for the other room a wish
from a god who wants one
circle of sweating men.

Do I know where to kneel and dig?
Will this desecration last a lifetime,
or will the weight of the blue fly
etched on this stone mean a theft,
a way of bowing down and tasting
the dirt as if water is not water
and greed is fed by shadows moving
to the other side of the eclipse?

GRANADILLA

Fruit of the passionflower in a secret room.
It has been a long time since a theory of illusion
was accepted by blue herons flying over the city.

Fruit of the exchange sliced into pieces geometrically
entering the body, nourishing the migration of butterflies
to be studied, but not tracked down in time.

Fruit of the flower mistaken for angels
and troubled monks who lick their fingers
of the sticky substance, go on with their task

of converting magic into dogma, the juice
of the fruit gathering in clay jars to become
the ballad of the body they were warned about.

Fruit of the harvest given its seed, its ecstasy promising
nothing to those desiring more than the pickings from
a trembling branch with its holy hair of the invisible.

Fruit in lavender glass bowls armed with moisture
from the laps of windows, mistaken for the divinity
of prophetic apples, bitten into by ripe ghosts full

of oranges, lemons, and darkening bananas—
yearning passed beyond the evil waters found
in the crushed fruit, the disappointment of finding

the pulp is dangerous overcome by emptying it
into the open mouth, this communion
between the hummingbird and its one prayer.

Federico García Lorca's Desk

It was tied with guitar strings
into a sack that held pigeon feathers,
the hair of lost dogs—cardboard
from a box of trinkets
he received from North Africa.
García Lorca's desk was a bundle
of things bearing down like an easy shot,
words recalled when discontent
was a shade of black,
coffee beans stolen in silence—
a clock over the hills waiting
for the next moon.

García Lorca's desk was a head
of lettuce, a bowl of goat soup,
the place where tiny hands
were named for their fingers,
ink spotting the pages to buy time
before three doors were slammed.
García Lorca's desk was his vow
to stir the rain with rootless awe,
then hide for years, come out
singing, reciting poems
from the warmth of laps,
paper flattened on the desk
so the sun could read.

García Lorca's desk was found
decaying in an empty field
where they lined him up,
the feathers falling out,
guitar strings rounding the sky
with wired light that sank
into the soft paper he used
to wipe his hands
before he was shot.

The Hawk Temple at Tierra Grande

I climbed the rocky slope and saw it—
the hawk temple in the trees,
feathers hanging on arrows
someone fired into the bark.

I came closer and found the hawk
perched there, waiting,
its black head the eye of the messenger,
its wings the color of my skin.

I stood under the tied trees,
wondered who did this—
why they lashed the mighty pines
together with rope,

binding the hawk to its perch,
leaving it there to blink
and stare at me as if
I was going to climb the tree.

I got too close and it tried
to fly, its talons cutting
into the branch, unable
to free itself from the rope.

I turned to run when I heard
a sound—a cry I hear to this day,
a motion of air to keep me
from saying what I do not say,

the sight of the hawk temple
not telling me if I will find
what I am looking for,
its screech not sounding
like it is going to be freed.

The blue stone in the palm of the hand.
The orange held between the breasts.
A hawk dead in the middle of the road.
The dry tree bursting through the adobe.

The half-burned church in Chamberino
blackened and open to the sky.
A field of cotton with two men running across.
The saint in the window.

The road to Cochiti and the pass
to the last desert town.
The red stone from the agate beach,
hundreds of seabirds disappearing
beyond the island of fog.

No one in the window.
The smell of chorizo frying in the air,
sound of a lone gunshot across the night.
The dog dead in the middle of the road.

The eagle flying above the car
outside the ruins at Abo.
A green stone worn around the neck
as the mango is sliced to be eaten.

The river drying, reappearing within hours.
An old woman carrying a broken wooden chair,
a hedge of enormous cactus blocking her house,
green and white streamers blowing on telephone poles.

The barbed wire surrounding the church.
A huge lizard on the fence at the rest stop.
The closed eyes of La Virgen.
A man mistaken for a ghost crossing the road.

The headlights of a distant tractor.
Hands rubbing a headstone again and again.
The lacquered shoes on the bookshelf from
a tiny baby who never made it.

I Am Afraid of the Moon

I am afraid of the moon when it comes down
to touch my throat, its light weaving
the white vein into my heart,
its brief cycle shimmering with evidence
that I have been wrong.

I am afraid of the moon when the toads
have become extinct, their legs deformed
into red spiders that drown their voices,
moonlight exploding in the water
to warn me I am still wrong.

I fear the full moon above the mountains,
its yellow wash the gold left behind by
men who loved night skies with stars,
their ancestors mistaken when they believed
there was no earth to flee to without
the light of their shadows falling into
their tombs to wash their toes.
That time the moon was wrong.

I do not trust the moon when
everything is gone, my companions from
the translucent land fleeing the cycles
of madness long ago, their terrible cries
beyond the seasons bringing them back
by the quarter moon where they try
to catch one dimension, but can't
separate it from the bloodless sky.

I am afraid of the moon because
it changes my home each time it arrives,
its dangling power ignored for a few nights
before the desert floor becomes a storm where
those of us blinded at birth by moonlight
don't know what it is like to be wrong.

FALLING INTO A FACE

It would be strange to fall into a face and never return.
That lone hawk chasing my car along
the mountain road would disappear.

How magnificent it would be
to fall into a face and be loved.
I could kiss the nipples of a startled girl

and know she would eventually love me.
I would be the first boy discovering the face
inside the face that prowls between

the joined bodies of two young lovers.
It would be here for me to fall
into a face and gain.

I would see how the world
is eaten by the rains that fall out
of the face that holds my face

in its hands, its cold fingers brushing
the water from my eyelids,
taking me deeper into the musk

I don't know—startled scent
of a face announcing the face
at the window is the same profile

that turns gently within the body,
moving out of the heart
as I fall into a face and see.

Kick the Heart

Kick the heart.
Kick the starting lance.
Throw the ground a word and stand back.
The color of terror is the envy
on body rags, the dragonfly war
scraped off a painting inside the door.

Kick the shame.
Kick the falling dawn as fortunate.
Throw the corrupted guest out the door.
A sequence of rhythms bound for
the light on your bed.
On the eggplant cooked for the husband
working late: an ant, a hair—
the only thing said to race the mind.
Take someone else's voice and touch their ears.
Make sure they hear you cry
in their own whispers, their harangue.

Kick the soil.
Kick the sweet drowning as if you know
the round jubilance of pear is afraid
of a darkening spoon, a honey of flavor,
the tender one who never touches your plate.
The tired one who rations food
to thank God eternity is here and there.

Slip the eye the blue-black stranger,
his instrument of scars and neglect,
its tune of every wish besides
the grave of a careless, quiet man.
Shape his sound into the thumb asking
for a ride in the years of not going anywhere.

Kick the alphabet.
Kick the hungry thigh and try again.
Reduce yourself to a moving mouth, a solemn happiness
that smells of the past, takes hold of the throat
and teaches you to despise omens—
ignore Apache mirrors on rock arches
as if you knew what their scratchings meant.

Kick the heart.
Kick the starting lance.
It moves deeper into the mouth of blinking neon
where vertigo is perfume, desire foaming
on your bare feet killed by frost,
taken by the animal waking inside your holy cross—
a figure of green gowns and things
that follows you until you dance.

Kick the truth.
Kick the belly until it confesses.
Admit you were fed by a woman
flapping in the wind, told to sit there by a father
who made her give birth to a shimmering head,
your brain of flowers blossoming upon
the body always first to confess.

What snow is left is tired water unmoved by your
seasonal words, your circle healing by slowing down,
swelling to the size of God,
yellow leaves in the blood nothing dangerous—
this impulse, this kick to the brittle lake
where the snow goes away.

What the Cottonwood Said

after James Wright

Don't witness the river changing course.
It is not good to stand here,

your mind crying—*This birth of mine
never came from the darkness.*

Don't measure the height of the clouds
with a dream. No one else

will cross the water without you.
Be there when my leaves dry up,

when the burlap sack full of shoes
drops under the shade of my trunk,

your missing pair floating down the current
to reach your resting place before you do.

*

Cottonwood shadows turning on me,
a sign was carved on your trunk.
When I carried you with me,
everything changed.

The freedom of the sparrows
and your huge, broken limbs.
If I stepped beyond your height,
there would be water—a way to explain.

My blessing is not a wish,
but the spice being tasted—
your leaves, their odor of silence.

I will not speak when I sample
the branch that falls at my feet.

Cottonwood closing the eyes of rivers,
there is a word or two about rain.
When I get wet, scars on your bark
are the clean breaks of a happy man.
How I wish it would rain.

This way of gaining two feet—
a steady hand on your lowest limb
as I listen to the swaying wind.
When I quit talking,
there will be your great height
and my childhood, again.

*

The tree is smiling.
This is before the invention of sleep.

When the lights in the neighborhood go out,
the tree smiles and I wait for the cool air

of early September to turn against me,
chill the hour beyond tomorrow

so I can watch the tree burn with age.
When the first orange leaves touch my face,

I wake and tell the truth:
The debut of shadows will pass beyond me.

One kind of cruelty enlarges the eyes.
There is this tree for order,

a beautiful thumb pressing
against the bark.

When the tree stops smiling,
the greater singing will have begun.

from
Cabato Sentora
1999

Calling the White Donkey

I called the white donkey that hurt my left shoulder
the last time it appeared, ramming me
with its ivory head, cracking my back
to relieve me of worry and hope.
I called the white donkey,
surprised at the sound of my voice.
Scared, I wondered if the white head
would give me its donkey brain,
snowy matter dripping into my ears
like the horse of the first man who fell off,
the donkey teaching me about desire
and the moan, that white hair on the back
of my head that warns me.

I called the donkey.
It came slowly toward me,
huge ears shaking with fury,
its breath turning the air white
as it bit into the white apple
of my throat.
I faced the donkey, watched
its gait become a shuffle of possession,
shaking its head as it stopped to
root its dirty hoofs in the ground.

I stepped back and clicked my fingers,
but it would not come closer, its snort
commanding I listen as it farted.
I walked away and did not know it was
I who yearned for labor of the ass
because the animal I summoned
couldn't remove the white scar from
my heart, a blind life I lived for good.

UNDER THE FREEWAY IN EL PASO

I hear streets light up
with secret weeping,

wish I could really hear it,
be given the owl in the rafters

and the road of veins
pulsing under the freeway

where the house of my birth
stands and decays.

Strangers have lived there
for the last forty-five years.

I have knocked on the door
and breathed inside the house.

Someone wants me
to disguise myself as a traffic

signal or a dark alley,
the imploded house across

from the last residence
of spirits who follows me inside.

Someone wants me to thrive
and surpass the disappearance

of my father, my dead grandfathers,
and my cousins who won't speak

to me because I come
from the house of candles,

rooms of saints, walls of glowing
crucifixes that broke the arms

of those who didn't believe
and cursed the smoke

that blew toward me,
the blankets I found inside

shattered rooms under
the freshly built freeway.

I went crazy with hope there,
restless as the prisoner

who fell down the hill,
impaled himself on yucca

and the turnpike of America,
that pointed staff of the priest.

I am the man who ate the catacombs
of honey in the walls of the house,

raised my lips to the hands that
took care of me inside the rooms,

taught me sweetness of prayer,
that stranger waiting for my return

so he could light the candles that didn't
melt in the many years of the passenger.

CABATO

Cabato—the art of tying sticks together with brown twine to make a secret symbol only the maker knows.

I tie eight sticks together, make sure
they look like the first star that fell at my feet.
The brown twine is tight, finished,
wound around the middle of the long,
smooth bamboo sticks.
It is not a star, but a falling diamond,
the closest pyramid that rose near
San Luis Potosi where my grandmother was born.

I make my cabato.
It has sixteen points resembling the cage of sorrows,
two feet long at its widest point,
a twisted wreath for those who want me
to tell them what it means.

I twirl my cabato in my hands,
a bamboo forest eliminated when
the first people found my grandmother,
gave her the will to live after letting go
of members of her family they didn't kill.

I hang my cabato on the wall, stiff vine
of what I always wanted to make.
The sticks remain.
The mutated star will dry into the wall
until the day I die.
I touch my cabato.
No one knows what I think
when I make sure the twine is secure,
the geometrical cross I have made a part
of the same tool invented by the first man
who tied anything together.

THE HAWK IN THE YARD

It stands in the grass the morning before Christmas,
its prey torn apart in its claws,
feathers scattered over the yard, piercing
yellow eyes staring straight ahead, in between
pecks at red meat that glistens in the sun.
Its white chest is streaked with brown markings,
a hawk in our yard surprising us by coming close,
eating as if something will be taken.
The hawk looks about and clutches the meat,
turns in the early light so I can see it,
not knowing I watch as it pulls a string
of intestine out of its catch,
tosses the tiny heart onto the grass,
these things sharp through my binoculars,
eyes of the hawk staring at what I can't
describe as it pecks and tears.

I look through the glasses, see a hawk surviving
in the frozen yard of a dying year, predator
taking a chance by landing in the yard,
weight of its prey forcing it here to eat.
The morning sun slashes across its wings
to show me there is no time for surprise.
Nothing will move or die without the hawk.
Nothing will be torn without reason,
no second chance to learn how a meal
is the defiant act of winter—the last ripping
of fear the hawk may be the wrong sign
because this hawk precedes the harvest,
but its pull at the meat must be a gift for
the new year, stark abundance dripping
as the hawk takes it in its claws and flies.

TWO STRIPED LIZARDS

They look like miniature orange and brown tigers
clinging to the concrete blocks in the backyard,

two lizards looking up at me as I lift the wood
off their hiding place.

They stick to the bricks, flatten themselves except
for their heads and enlarged eyes, tiny faces

looking curious and human, staring at me
when I move, blinking as if I was going to grab them,

one of them springing out of the brick, disappearing
into the grass to lead me away from their home.

Two striped lizards is a good omen for the man
who knew the reptiles that led him to the well.

Two striped lizards are signs of abundant thirst,
plenty of water, their rapid movement and caution

leaving me with something to grasp—a blade of grass,
an abandoned spider web, a concrete block I won't move

because I learned what the striped lizard means—
a tiger in the canyon is as good

as the escaped dragon of the heart—
the second lizard not moving

as I leave it alone and close the lid
on the muffled source of its trembling.

THE FINGER MOTH

The finger moth alights in the shadows
of what has been—brushes my knuckles
with the right to be defeated by
the kissing beauty of my hands.
The finger moth folds into the century
where love will be a mountainside,
the fluttering inside my farthest reach.

The finger moth dissolves into
the verdict of my eyelashes,
moves in and out of the shadows,
lands on the chair where my father
wished for nothing, sat in his T-shirt
and drove himself out of the light.

The finger moth is petrified
in the bathroom mirror, but
where are the men to show me
mirrors always sit in front
of shaving men?

The finger moth cuts itself
into the glass, tattoos its shape
out of lines and codes of wings.
When I turn to leave the room,
it is night and the moth answers.
I can't go because there is
something for me to breathe.
The finger moth explodes into
a clattering of threads, blinding
prisms there and not there.
I can't depart until the finger moth
is gone like the chair my father

carved, its wooden legs trembling
under my face in the mirror,

the room welcoming the shadows
with nothing unexpected, no light
to wash my hands clean
as they reach for the moth.

FROM THE FACE

Each night the Gila monster enters
the house of the daughter,
lies down in the exception of water
and disappears for fifty years.

Each morning the hanged man comes
down off the tree and enters the town,
the whispers memorized, his footsteps
sounding like his children forgive him
and finally call him "father."

Each evening the blind crosses are torn off
the church walls, then piled in a tower
that never falls until the tired ones
stop breathing and ignite the flames.

Each night the horizon praises its beauty
and disappears, arrives at dawn before
the stricken country sees the threat
of mountains lying between one storm
and the one morning flower.

THE ANGELS OF JUÁREZ, MEXICO

Sometimes they save people from drowning in the river.
Their faces are the color of the water,
wings soaked in the oil of crossing and
keeping them from leaving the border.
The oldest angel is a man from the last century
whose white hair hangs to the ground.
He floats above the water each time he saves
a *mojado* who tries to cross in the raft,
falling into the current to be somebody.

The angels of Juárez look over the *colonias,*
nibble on the cardboard shacks like the rats
they never fear because rats have their own angels.
When children fall into the poison waters,
the angels dance above the glowing waves,
pull out the chosen child with a kiss and
toss him on the bank for others to find.

These angels know about revolution and dying,
prefer to hover over the Rio Grande
where the bodies move at night,
fighting for air some angles mistake
as a grasp toward heaven.

The angels of Juárez sometimes hide
from the desire to cross, hesitate
to take a chance and send a chant
over the dirty waters, the latest
drowning victim wondering
why the tired old man he was told
to look for, never extended a hand.

The angels appear in the night,
listen to the crush of water as the course

of the border tightens with searchlights
and the hidden green cars of patrol.
They swim over the electricity,
wings humming to create a magnet
that makes it easier to cross.

The angels don't know
something is going to end.
They don't appear near the churches,
the missions, or the kneeling altars.
They are not part of the prayer,
the ritual, or the escape.
They know the river is moving faster,
churning toward the horizon
that accepts fewer souls each year.

The angels hover to make sure
the water keeps flowing,
mud of the barefoot moving
to the other side of the river where
no angels dwell because this side
was cleared of faith long ago,
waiting streets of El Paso never
mistaken for the place of angels.

WHITE

Written after several treks through White Sands National Monument, New Mexico, site of Trinity, the first atomic bomb explosion, 1945. My parents were in high school at the time and told me El Pasoans, that day, saw a white flash in the sky one hundred miles to the north.

The White Silence

The white silence is absolved.
It murmurs in the body and heaves.
It sees me and arms itself with warmth.
The white silence is a reward
worth the wet hair and the angry eye.
It shifts into a love for tears and windows.
The white silence is feeding,
thinks of me coming back talking,
but to talk would be a white noise from
white flowers I stepped on long ago.

The White Iguana

The white iguana sits on my wife's head.
Its tail covers her eyes.
She can't know I am coming back.
The white iguana prays on the head
of the woman I have loved for years.
When I open my eyes, the iguana hisses,
combs the hair of my wife with its claws.
When my wife opens her eyes,
the white iguana loves the light,
leaps off her head and flies.

The White Tarantula

The white tarantula crawled out of my heart,
moved down my chest and brushed my nipples.
The white tarantula visited me in my sleep.
When I woke, it waited, hidden somewhere in the room.
When I woke, I had crossed to the other side.
The white tarantula denies it came out of my heart.
When I search for it in my room,
its absence tells me it is back in my blood.

The White Tree

The white tree grew at my window.
One night, I heard someone climb its branches.
When I went to look, a white shadow crossed
itself, then disappeared.
In two days, the white tree died.
The first night of its decay, I could not sleep.
The white tree shed its light.
When I sat up in bed, its leaves were singing
and changing color in the air.

The White Hair

I found the white hair sticking to my shirt.
When I plucked it between two fingers,
I saw it was the hair that grew on my head.
I found the white hair was twisted, tiny knots
bending its fiber like a line on a map.
When I looked in the mirror, my entire head was white.
I dropped the white hair in surprise.
It disappeared as it hit the floor.
When I looked in the mirror, my entire head was black.

The White Guitar

The white guitar was stolen from my closet.
When I found it was gone, music came through the walls.
I went into the other room, but no one was there.
The white guitar had twelve strings,
given to me by my father before he died.
I played it only once, the day before I left.
I thought I could touch what had already been sung,
but I hid the guitar in the closet for years.
Then, it was stolen.
When I open my doors, I still hear
the strumming and there is a song.

The White Fountain

The white fountain sprays a mist over the streets,
shoots higher and all is cold.
The white fountain collects coins and wets the dog,
soaks me when I walk.
The white fountain blinds me when I pause,
water rising from the thirst for love.
The white fountain is a cloud that cleans me,
freezes in midair when I have a name.

The White Room

I found it in my fiftieth year.
The white room opened and shared its furniture.
When I entered, I found a huge bed
the size of desire.
The white room was empty, but kept me.
When I sat in the white chair, I thought of plants.
When I lay on the cold bed, I had no words.
The white room kept me fifty years.
When I rose to leave, I had no ideas.
When I touched the doorknob, the windows opened.

The White Sirens

The white sirens called when the city burned.
They shattered my ears and gave me hope.
I walked the streets and saw white buildings.
The white sirens shrieked with hope.
I hid in the alleys and waited for smoke.
The white sirens showed me the way.
When they rose in a deafening sword,
I found the shoe in the trash can.
The white sirens drove me out of town.
When I listened, I heard the wailing,
the cry to look up at the radiating sky.

The White Cars

The white cars followed me into September.
They were everywhere like crickets.
When I hid in the barrio, headlights danced.
When I crossed the street, I was the traffic.
The white cars were full of gasoline.
They waited at intersections, engines thriving.
When I thought of waving one down, I cried.
The white cars followed me into the world.
When I recognized one driver, he was my father
in his Navy uniform, back from the war.

The White Streets

I walk the white streets in search of fame,
find nothing but white dirt in my socks.
Signs on street corners spell God in Spanish.
The white streets have no lanes,
lead to the white desert,
but the desert is no longer there.
I watch boys fight on asphalt and let them gain.
I cross and cross and never get lost.

The white streets have no seasons.
I return from white dunes and am touched.
I return on them and no one knows,
come back to be greeted by a glowing, white cross.

Lifted White

They told me to lift my head and watch
the sun kiss the radiating century goodbye.
I lifted my soul instead and was blinded
by the flash my spirit released.
They told me to let go of my past
so I could see how many miracles
I could find in the fever of loneliness.
I gave them my history instead,
was blessed with knowing how many years
it would take to say, "I am no longer afraid."

They told me to embrace the child
on either side of my path, listen
to their weeping as if it was my own.
I told them to sing, instead,
gave them years to end their songs.
When they let go of my hands,
I was too old to understand.

Thinking the century was over,
I lay down to die.
When I opened my eyes,
I was still there and saw
the white light was one god
with one hand, pulsing his defiant veins.

BROWN POT

And so I eat from a brown pot,
sticking my fingers into

the stomach of the seed,
smearing them with laughter

and the growling voice.
I eat the brown eye, its carving

pupil leaving my sight
to enter ladders of fingers—

mistaken bellies of hungry fools.
And so I eat from a brown hand,

opening the leaves to fill the room—
odors, smells, gases from the juice

my father extracted when he fried
a goat and called it God.

I eat from a brown pot,
greasy sides glistening with words

I first learned when I was full—
like "Mama, Papa, stand up."

I spit the stem from the woven heart
and swallow the chasing worm,

mutation of protein
and the tired tooth,

making me taste digested truth
that escapes the wind no man

calls his own without a name.
And so I sit and belch, wishing

the picked bone was used
to trace lines on my face,

the way the cook cut her hands
and fed the pot to make it brown.

I eat from a forgotten brain—
scooping thoughts out of the skull,

licking the bone to see again as I
listen for the hum of the tongued ear.

I eat from the first body, asking
for crumbs to come alive,

change hunger into the shape
of smoked-out rooms where women

chanted and cooked fear into
a *masa* to shape the man, take him

into the world for years to come.
And so I eat from a brown pot

on the greasy table, fill myself
with chewing voices, shards of

clay sticking in my throat, my
deepest swallowing before stuffing

myself with the livers of what
should have been fed to me.

Beyond Having

And, always, there is desire like
the orange and banana changing
texture on the kitchen shelf.
Their skins sink slowly into themselves.
There is the liquid of lust and thirst,
an open gloss of choice and cutting,
a lying down toward the wind,
the heaving you were warned about.

And, soon, there is love like
miniature spellings embedded in the shoulder,
waiting to be misspelled and washed,
brought back by perception that fades
with what moves below the arm,
hinging on a doubt cried away.
There is the mistake of giving name
to the prune, the print bitten off
and covered over by black hair
whose numbers are kept secret,
long strands in the tale of the carpet,
the pomegranate and the hundred
ways of staying there.

And, besides, there is danger of riding desire
until it carves you into its swollen throat,
steel-cry of possession and the infinite blessing
of fingers missing from the first time,
fingernails tracing the shape of the strawberry
to memorize roughness without leaving.
There is the flavor and the understanding,
a place to rest the eye after traveling,
a force that binds you together
without you knowing red marks
on your back are places where wings
would have risen if you were an angel.

THE HEAD OF PANCHO VILLA

The rumor persisted that the head of Pancho Villa
disappeared on its own before they buried him,
found its way across the Chihuahua desert to El Paso
where he killed several men and kept women.
The head floated across the Rio Grande,
snapping turtles diving out of its way,
the brown mass moving on its own, his thick hair
and moustache shining in the green water.

The skull of the general evaporated in the heat,
only to reappear at the church door,
the early man who came to pray startled by
the bullet holes between the closed eyes.
He stared at the head, then ran.
When he brought the sleepy Padre to look,
they only found a wet spot on the ground
before they bowed and crossed themselves.

The rumor ran that the head became
the mountain surrounding the town.
Others said it was the skull that sat for years
on the highway west to Arizona.
It was true because my grandparents lived there,
told their children the skull glowed
on the roads, until my grandfather died
and his family returned to the other mountain.

I see the head of Villa each time I drive into El Paso.
It rises off the setting sun as the evening turns red.
By now, I am convinced the eyes are open, the hair longer.
After all, the moon is enough when I turn to take a look.

At the Rio Grande near the End of the Century

See how the cottonwood bends at the waist.
　　It turns gray, cracking as the sun goes down.
There is no limit to returning.
　　See the trunk turn toward what has changed you.

When you place yourself against the river you can't reach,
　　it is an old habit draining your hands of strength.
Look at the cottonwood disappearing.
　　Its hidden sediment is alighting out of your reach.

It is not water.
　　It was not made to mark the border with leaves.
Only the river can cease its mud and turn its brown heart.
　　Only the passage belongs to swollen, bare feet.

What you know is the scent of the desert you are so tired
　　of writing about,
how it covers the past and hangs as the ember of thought—
　　wisdom molded out of the falling world.

What you love is removed from the pale circle of shadows.
　　It will never return. It will weep.
Even the moisture in the armpit smells like the trees.
　　Tomorrow you will see another kind of growth.

See the threads of the hills turning back the revolt.
　　See how the men are crossing the river toward you.
When the cottonwood petrifies in the lone spot,
　　history will be overlooked and you will die.

What you keep are the thousand miles of the wounded breast.
　　What you smell is the fine cotton of the dying tree.
When the white balls stick to your hair, listen to the fleeing men.
　　Even their backs are wet and some of them look like you.

from
The Heat of Arrivals
1996

Watching a Film of Van Gogh on Christmas Eve

The madness of the ear listening
to the silence of the sunflowers
makes us wait for Christmas to pass
so we can return our gifts,

smear our hands and faces with paint,
go beyond the memory of the crude angel
wanting freedom impossible on canvas.

*

Van Gogh scrawls "I am the whole spirit"
on his studio wall, screams
as he drinks the turpentine,
yells for his brother Theo

who exhibits paintings to a world
that doesn't know the creator buys time
with canvas nailed to the broken wood,
frames he rips as he stumbles in a field of crows.

*

Days ago, I was asked by someone
to speak on the difference between spirit and soul.
I had myself photographed,
the picture revealing too much,
its light separating white from black.

It shows a man standing without his glasses,
wondering why the photographer chose
my bare features few have seen,
a profile emerging out of a negative
with the artist's chemical burning
brown skin upon my blinded face.

Van Gogh tears sunflowers off their stalks,
kicks the canvas, staggers across the horizon
to find himself in front of the mirror,
blue and yellow paint coagulating on his lips.
He tastes the brush, then screams
into the mirror of comprehension as he slices his ear.

Hymns rise when we recall
where we were on this night years ago.
We ate bread for the birth that exhausts
our beliefs in getting there.

It was our swallowing of the paint in secret,
washing our mouths and hands,
until we were empty on Christmas Eve,
yet filled with a yearning we ignored for years.

We waited for something to happen—
a photo to reveal the instant the camera clicked
and the crows vanished in the sunflowers,
returned the canvas to dirt.
We shredded it as we dived into
Van Gogh's mirror of Christmas stars
and never came back,
the abandoned yellow field proof
this is the difference between spirit and soul.

THE EAGLE IN THE ASHES

a dream

Walking down the alley toward
my grandmother's house where I grew up,
I see trees, lawns and houses in the barrio
breathing a fine layer of ashes,
mounds of gray powder piled
against the torn fence.

Five giant eagles rise out of it,
enormous birds with brown faces
of long-haired, silent men.
Without flapping their wings,
they step down the mound,
strong-taloned feet sinking
in the fine dust.

Each eagle walks past me
without saying a word,
their long, black hair swirling,
bronze faces proud and knowing,
feathers shining in the ashes.

They jump onto the wire fence,
then land in the yard.
One by one, they walk into
my grandmother's house.
I stand by the gate,
sift ashes through my fingers,
rub my hands together
before climbing the mound,
trying to get over the fence,
slipping down and getting up,
trying to open the gate.

IN THE TIME OF THE SCORPION

I found the scorpion crawling near my foot
and knew it was time to die,
fresh out of high school in June,

my room in my parent's house the only place
I could write my first poems,
the scorpion the only visitor I had at night.

I shook it away from my foot with a pencil
and it sprang for the wall.
I turned off the lamp to light a candle,
its flickering motion spreading to the scorpion.

I stepped closer, watched it become
a drop on the wall, bloodstain of a long future,
erect tail poised to sting the clear vision
I had back then.

*

I know the scorpion as it descends
onto the marks on my back
where it strikes.

When I see the scorpion,
it breathes under my skin,
shows me where to lie down and
wait for its dozen babies to emerge
from the tips of the night thorns.

*

The scorpion came apart under the knife.
I saw the wheel of poison grow into the drop
we would love to smear into our eyes,
be able to see where it came from,

where we anoint our eyes
with what survives,
bitter our fingertips for
the root and the spring.

The tiny globe emerged to spill
over the torn body and endless legs,
coat it with desire to fight back,
yellow oozing over my blade
like a human face emerging
on the dying scorpion.

*

The myth of the scorpion comes to me
to catch the storm over my skin,
fly with the fast creature,

trail under the rocks to wait,
lift the stone and pick up the stick
to spell a bite in the sand.

I go back to the old house and enter
the room, find the screen on the window still there,
hardened drops on the wire proving
the myth scorpions glow in the dark.

*

The time of the scorpion is near.
Humidity no longer hides its form
in the black corners of the room,
signals the summer of being stung.

My blood refused to come out that night.
I knew how to take the red scorpion,
jump out of the way
of the wetness inside,
find what it was like to go down.

Sueño de Mexico

after a painting by José Clemente Orozco 1926

Cortés y La Malinche

A dead body at their feet,
Cortés y la Malinche sit up naked
after fucking for the third time.
She sits with eyes closed,
long black hair braided behind her,
large nipples brushed by
the conquistador's right arm.
Cortés shields her against death,
pushes her dark-red body onto the bed.

He stands tall and pale,
heavy legs stepping over the dead body
of a man who couldn't reach them.
Cortés creates the first mestizo of the New World.
No one knows why he chose her
as he thrusts into the woman,
the latest earthquake rumbling
across the temple when he grunts
and says everything is settled.

Juárez

Once, stumbling drunk in the *mercado* of Juárez,
I saw the young whore emerge
from behind the vegetable crates.
She seemed to be in a heroin daze,
emerging from a customer's rape.
Her eyelids were painted in
black mascara to match
black lipstick on her mouth.

She motioned to me to stop,
black fingernails pointing at me
in the stinking tomatoes and goat meat.

I moved back, stared at the *turistas*
who pushed her so they could get
to the bargain of leather belts.
I kept walking toward the bridge,
but couldn't forget the sight of her
falling to her knees.

I reached the crossing as she reminded me
of the straw doll I found floating
in the Rio Grande, long ago.
Someone threw its gnarled face
into the river.
I made it to the bridge,
recalled how I tossed the doll back,
its warped wood sliding through
my fingers like the young whore
disappearing in my haste to get away.

Cathedral

I climbed the ancient tower
of the cathedral of La Virgen de Guadalupe,
the oldest church in Juárez.
I wanted the myth to be true.
If you opened the south window,
you would face the spot on the mountain
where the padres buried the gold.

I climbed the suffocating, wooden stairs,
narrow rock chamber going straight up,
creaking under my weight,
three-hundred-year-old stones
smelling of forgiven sins.
I climbed to answer the dare

of my high school friends who waited
in the quiet sanctuary below,
trying not to draw attention,
three of us drinking and wandering
around the crowded plaza.

I reached the top, pushed
wooden shutters open to the heavy air.
I stared at the mountains of El Paso miles away,
as if I knew where to look,
spotted a gleam of light in the distance,
so I could be the one to tell my friends
where we should dig for treasure.
I turned around, dizzy, breathing hard,
the confining cell forcing me back.

An old woman stood there,
tight against the railing,
her thin figure draped in dirty rags,
gray hair falling beyond the stairs,
covering a face she wouldn't show.
I looked again and she was gone,
but could smell her presence,
taste the difference in the swallowing air.

I almost fell down the stairs,
got down to find my friends gone.
I made it to the bridge alone,
lost for a few blocks, knowing
the woman in the tower followed me,
nudged me as I reached the checkpoint,
her invisibility marking the last time
I would cross, the beam
on the mountain I would forget
because there were others who
had already seen the flame
from up there.

Rattlesnake Dance, Coronado Hills, 1966

after the photo "Hopi Snake Dance" by Edward Curtis

Snakes in the mouth.
From the ground to the mouth,
to the sky, dancers curl in a circle
to gather snakes,
carry them in their mouths.

They dance for rain,
faces painted like blind snakes
of the firstborn, the ones that can't see,
yet sense where the heart moves,
where to strike after the rain dance.

*

I climb up the steep arroyo,
listen for the buzzing,
a boy of fourteen looking for the rattler
I spotted the day before.
Its quickness behind the rocks becomes
a stillness along the dirt walls,
a sign there is nothing there,
until I trip and roll a few yards down,
laughing, calling to my friends to come up,
not knowing they ran when they heard it
because I climbed too far.

*

Women and children watch
the dance from the high walls.
Only the men can gather the snakes
in their arms and mouths.
Only the men can pick them up

and wear them like new arms and legs
coming rapidly alive,
quick appendages crawling into
the body to make it whole.

*

I found it nailed to the wooden fence,
the rattle cut off, its skin peeled back
and left hanging in the breeze.
Stiff patterns blew like paper
with an unknown alphabet burned in blood.
The killer left the skin as a god exposing
the fate of snakes to those who follow them.

The flat, wrinkled head dripped
its beauty into the wood,
pure instinct beaten back
before it could kiss the follower,
brand him with the wisdom that fire
must enter the body,
wash it of desire and breath and
swell it to the size of dying,
shape it into a form this one can't take
as I pull it off the fence.

*

One dancer bends over,
grabs two rattlers in one hand,
his grace in the sun a stain in the photo,
his disappearance in the moving circle
a sign the snakes coiled into the bone of song
like muscles given and granted,
flutes of rain spitting at the red sky that falls
around the tight chests of the exhausted men.

*

After killing three of them,
I saw the fourth climb up the porch,
squeeze into the bricks to disappear
into a corner of the house.
Its sleek body vanished into the wall,
became a part of our home.

I never saw it again, but lay awake at night,
knowing it was inside the house,
trapped between wood and mortar,
moving from room to room without rattling.
It waited for me to press my hands
above my bed, push in the dark,
tap and push the wall that smothered
every breath I took as I waited.

*

The dancers run and chant,
faster and faster,
dozens of snakes crossing their feet,
falling off painted bodies,
blending into the hair and masks,
clinging to their necks as
the dancers hold each other.

The circle grows smaller as
snakes fly through legs,
women and children staring from above,
the pit of dancers growing deeper,
the round floor of the earth collapsing
to let men and snakes go their way,
choose how much blood to let per beat,
how much blood, per rattle,
to spit into the starting rain.

THE GRANDFATHER

The grandfather goes down to the lanterns
and lights the stars.

He takes his bottle and recalls the rattler
he killed to make way for the family.

The grandfather shaves in the morning,
cuts his throat at night.

The blossom of what he knows
spills against the years of healing,

of going down
to the railroad lanterns

to light his aching arms and legs
with the ointment of his scars.

SNAKESKIN

a dream

I thought the rattler was dead
and I stuck my finger in its mouth,
felt the fangs bite down,
penetrate me without letting go,
the fire removing my eyes,
replacing them with green light
of the reptile illuminating my hand.

It entered my bone and blood,
until my whole body was green and damp,
my whole left side turning
slick and cool as I tried
to pull it out of my body.

I peeled my skin back to find
my veins were green and held
tightly what I believed,
what forced itself into me
and allowed itself to be given
without knowing I carried that secret,
as I crawled over the ground,
became sinew the sun steps on.

I leaned against a huge boulder,
sweated, waited, slept.
By morning, I found a new way
of embracing that rock,
new life in the green flesh
of the world.

NEVER

SAM

I never worked on car engines
with my father.

We never saw the mechanics
of the world or shared

a joke about the deep
losses between men.

We never ate a meal together,
just the two of us,

never identified stars in the sky
as witnesses to our longing,

our wrestling and shuffling to embrace
like drunk bears colliding with trees,

alone in the thick forest
of our separate dreams.

The Energy of Clay

Brown dirt embeds itself,
sparks a dream out of my fingers.
I sink them into the moisture,
        fall off the cliff to find my father
at the bottom, molding
clay figures of my mother, our house,
as rain washes it away,
covering him with gray mud
of the one who creates.

        I smear the clay across my forehead,
paint my face as the son sleeping
in the soil to find wanderings of the blood,
gloves of mud cracking into the palms
we follow when we shape our sculpture
of dirt and hair cut from
clay coming out of the heart
of the statue of my father.

My mother once said,
"When you drink from the jar,
you can taste the desert."
        She looked for grains of dirt,
chips of the inner jar in water.
"Crunch the dirt in your teeth
and you taste the earth."

We drank from the jar,
inhaled the smell of cold water
like an underground spring we dared dig up,
earthy taste of the jar filling us with need
        to go down deeper, settle into the cave
like we had no choice—
our thirst meant we were fated to go under,

never look up at the sky,
always down to the ground where jars sprang
like brown wombs of the mother giving us
the first taste of clay.

I come up, roll the dirt,
praise the clay for being so pure,
sharper and hotter than the form I tried to shape.
I pound it like the last traveler afraid water
will not help him.
I push my palms together.
The desert emerges from my oozing hands.

I push my palms together.
The face of my father falls into the plant.

I push my palms together.
The face of the sweetness of earth takes shape
from the clay ruins.

I push my palms together.
The desert expands to cover us.
The face of clay melts in the canyons.

Of the family, I know little.
They left to dig where the clay comes up
alive, perfect for the fingers
where moisture seeps and
obeys the masked hands.

Of my father, he lives in two worlds—
land of the digger and the cave of clay,
territory he never inhabits because
his houses were built from harder ground,
mixture of the bitter cottonwood and the thorn,
formed with the isolation of walls where all fathers,
in their son's clay, lie down to forget.

ODE TO THE FAMILY OF SPIDERS

I hide behind the house, hear the cries
of my mother looking for me,
summer evening turning black as her anger,
cold as the side of the house where I crouch
watching the swamp cooler drip black
widow spiders on the ground.

They fall like black marbles, disappear
as eyeballs rolling toward the tomb,
huge, fat spiders falling out of the swamp
cooler as my mother shouts my name,
not knowing I hide to descend into
the safety of spiders where I find
a web at age four, bend as small as
the spiders carrying secrets the way
I carry what I did wrong into the slippery grass.

I crouch for over an hour,
my knees caked in mud,
black widows emerging to surround me,
unaware I would touch them if
I knew how the body eats itself,
if I was old enough to know
my mother's search is the unweaving of
the strands as they stick to my fingers.

I would touch the spiders if
I was sure their bite brought me
closer to the wet puddle of young men
who gather as boys, learn to crawl
toward voices in the dirt until it is safe
to get up and go back into the quiet house.

*

Raking soaked yellow leaves,
I uncover three hibernating spiders.
Looking closer, I see
they are brown recluses,
their liquid frozen in sleep,
their slow bodies barely moving,
legs vibrating to come alive.

I must destroy them
before they go into the house,
worried they could bite someone.
I think about how they say
brown recluses eat your flesh
into a steak-size wound.

I should kill them
before they turn me
into the digging man
who grabs moist ground
to bring everything
back to life,
his body shaking
with cold harvest,
brown recluses wriggling
like small stars that secretly

fell to burn with the digger's
desire to cover his tracks
without stepping on them,
as their pointed legs mark
the spot where he spit
into the boiling sand
in agony.

*

Five daddy long-legs on the ceiling
wait for me to turn off the light

so they can move around the bed.
I dream of being surrounded by webs,

a guest of a wise, old poet
with a house built by spiders.

Five of them explore my body as I sleep,
move like miniature ferris wheels across the bed.

In my dream, I am captured and taken
to the corner of the room where I lose

my vision to the sleeping song
of patient spiders where

I stay ahead of the daddy long-legs
by hiding in the room,
under the trees where spiders leave a sign,
a thin, white symbol woven
on my snoring head,
its course the thread to another life,

a chance of reaching out
with the bitten, swollen hand.

Late Night Moon

after Galway Kinnell

The moon closes its eyes,
   bends into the eastern territory,
      its frozen music the numb sound
         never granted, a collision opening a passage.

Once more, the rains polish
   my trance with an electric skin
      where lightning hits, allow the ground to sink.
         The huge space of doubt settles over
      the geometry of what I have been.

Past the imprint of the hours,
   in the moving night sparks,
      there are impossible notions in finding
         the arrow stuck in the rapid eye of my skull.

It hurtles faster as it pierces
   the embers toward what I should have been
   when the moon hit the glass.

*

The night listens.
   These have to be the wages of love,
      knowing too much without taking the clot
         out of the beat, the dance out of the blood.

I close the book, see the photo
   of the "life mask" as the man holds it to the light,
      its closed eyes far from what he knows,
         eyelids like the ones I opened
            when I molded the mask out of wood.

January moons continue to fade.
  The night rhymes with the hush I hate.
    The moon releases the man and the woman
      so they have another night to believe in each other,
        another late moon over their first quiet house.

I get up, go to the window and see how the cold
  reminds me of the respected dead hanging from trees
    like bodies of natives burned by custom,
      as if this calling stirs sound in this sleeping house,

as if I know what it means to suspend belief
  from the great tree I wish would fall
    over my wife and my house to protect us.

I want to slip around the tree, a lover wanting
  the limbs to unfasten a role he accepted
    when moonlight was metal on his arms.

Moonlight was the kiss the two of them missed,
  knowing the glow was meant to destroy their doubts,
    a reminder this arc measures how far they go
      as the moon rocks them past sleep.

When the paws enter the house,
  my eyes close to avoid the fire that follows,
    a white globe hurting in my shoulder blade
      as I turn and hold her, admitting the bodies

that don't know what the moon does to them
  are part of the motions and tides
    where I wake to begin.

THE MAGNETS

on turning forty

They draw me closer like the hands
of one grandmother I kissed upon
visiting her in the barrio.
The magnets make me look at my waist,
wonder why the ache is in the street,
houses giving off stinking air,
a magnetic field collecting old newspapers,
broken-down cars, alleys where
the drummer cowers before he beats
on his bag of beer cans.

I visit the irrigation canal that
churns green and flows beyond the streets,
wait for the alligator to swim by,
the one released from the plaza long ago.
I feel the pull toward the mongrel dog,
the clicking of the magnets in the church,
an attraction for open doorways.

*

I remove the magnet from my neck,
a medal of a denied saint.
I will never witness the migration of bats again,
stand at the entrance of the caverns
as bats shoot out of the opening,
the evening bristling with their intelligence.

The sky bruises against the horizon
of yucca plants erect as magnets
surrounding the cavern,
miles of yucca encircling the poles
to protect them from the wind
that pulls me into the hole.

*

He tells me to believe what I have seen,
insists magnetic force comes from the blade,
the woman wanting us to keep something for her.
He says magnets are missing metals
from an underground wound,
a husband's wrist broken by a slammed car hood,
loyal dance of an old couple watching the street.

He says tortillas and menudo attract flies.
He learned red chili kills all life,
insists magnets let him sleep fulfilled,
delicious food he fixes
long after his wife has died.

He cries that the magnets get stronger
when he peels the pods to find no difference
in the seeds of hunger and the seeds of love.

*

I climb the rocks because the minerals are there,
ascend to where I buried the seashell,
rusted can, and pencil twenty-eight years ago.
I reach the rocks because I am allowed one mountain,
climbing to readjust the magnets.
Then, I stand and look down.

I clear my chest of a fist encountered up here,
set my foot on the humming slab.
I move to survive when I touch my heart.
I climb higher before deciding to bend and dig.

from
Railroad Face
1995

THE BELL

I stole a bird whistle from the store,
gave a nickel to my crying sister.
I hid under the bed when my father came home.
I ate alone and went to sleep,
awoke in the middle of the night and knew no one.

In the front yard, a bird dropped a tiny bell
from its claw as it hovered over our willow tree.
The bell hung on a branch for years,
but I never knew it tinkled on the wind.

I stole another bird whistle and blew it.
The bell shivered and fell off the tree.
I never heard it, saw it, or picked it up.
Anything can be.

Before the Facts

The mushroom in your mouth was
an animal hidden in the flesh of the soil.
When you swallowed it,
you quit believing in sin.

The singing knives of the clown
are marks on your back left there
by the fists of your father.
When he paints his grinning mask on,
you laugh because you belong to him.

The naked mother in the mouth of the bird
is an idea you have imagined
resting in your lap, fear you will be
discovered speaking to droplets
of water that have kept you alive.

The pears sitting inside the carved bottle
are the crucifix of your escape.
When you deem them eatable wood,
your jealousy is infinite and tragic.
It is the pears turning brown like your eyes.

The constant, splendid frame of your house.
The misremembered moist air.
The moment of softly placing your mouth.

RAILROAD FACE

I sit with my railroad face and ask God to forgive me
for being a straight line toward the dead
who were buried with their poor clothes
in the Arizona desert of iron borders.

This way of waving to the embers of the past,
not apologizing for carrying torn rosaries inside
my pockets where beads of worry became fossilized
insects whose dry husks I kept since a child.

Faces adopted me from boys who hated their parents.
I was told not to repeat this,
reminded by the priest who unmasked himself.
I was told there was a great horror down
the hallway of the smelly Catholic school.
Once, my friend Joey jumped off the second floor window
and flattened his brains over the asphalt yard.

I see a hibiscus blossom.
It is a bright yellow flower that lasts one day.
Its shape brings tears, saves me from the hummingbird
that dots the air with patterns resembling an alphabet
too familiar to smell like a railroad worker.

I love heaven when I admit the spikes
and the railroad ties came from
the labor of fate and not the labor of love.
The tracks are my cross.

The tiny car is full of sweating men.
They look into the eye of the sun,
hold their hammers over their blackened heads.
If staring grows in the common search,
a perfume dots the heart with greed.
Silence between the lightning of pounding stakes.

Once, I rode the train home
to see if the smoke from the speeding engine
was going to enter my lungs.
I never wore the old, yellow hat of the crew,
but returned the shovel and the bag of railroad spikes,
thought I saw my grandfather, the foreman, running
across the desert in overalls, changing his skin
from brown to the black of the scorched engine.

I live with my railroad face, its smoothness hammered
by sweating crews that knew the line of hot iron
was going to end in the west someday.
I live with my railroad face and don't know why
the tracks disappear on the horizon.
I cross my railroad face and comb my hair.

DISGUISE

In the past, I had no choice.
It was a narrow star.
    It flew over my head like the sparrow
my father warned me about.

It was only a star.
A light.
    A flash across the desert that changed me.

In the past, I had two eyes.
One was blinded by the star.

    The other grew sharper,
able to see into the dust storm
when it was time to collect sticks.

I had two eyes that served me.
I could see half-blind,
    half there.

Years later,
    I see with both eyes.

    My vision is clear and simple.
No scar.
    Now, the muscles in my legs hurt.

There are two sources of light:
    One is my slowing heart.
        The other is the flame I saw
when I flapped my hands like the sparrow
    and touched my eyes.

*

The particles of this language heal the walker.
Enter my body.

The grains of dirt in his hair spell something.
Enter my body.

Once I heard my parents calling my name.
Enter my body.

Once I never answered, the desire went away.
Enter my body.

When the neck of the wood cross breaks.
Enter my body.

The view from the corner of the mountain is a lie.
Enter my body.

Once I dreamed I was seaweed and had no head.
Enter my body.

I have swallowed wax and consumed ashes.
Enter my body.

I have denied the existence of bread.
Enter my body.

I bit the spoiled leaf for the first time.
Enter my body.

In the past, I had two eyes.
Enter my body.

Now, there are two sources of light.
Enter my body.

*

On the first night, a spirit loves me a little,
then vanishes.
On the second, I am able to speak to my father.
How do I know his beard?
Reaching for my stepson, he is gone.
Looking for the boys in the street, I am gone.

Can I hate the sound of God punishing me?
Can it be a stillness, a breath, a prayer?
In my wife's garden, a hummingbird
hovers above a red wasp.
On the ground, a white rock with a crater
cupped out of it.
The other day, I went crazy
and knew I had to run.

Where I came from, you can walk home.
Where I have lived, you can frighten a bird
or two and be disturbed.
How do I accept the church in place of the kiva?

*

Inside the church, a music eats itself.
There is no time to recall language.
It has to do with smelling the incense
and denouncing the existence of bread,
crossing the sanctuary as a child and
reaching the altar as an old man.

*

In four directions
there are four countries.

I came from all of them.
I had only one name.

I left one country
when I was born.

I never entered the second,
but I was there.

The third gave me time
to find a house and street.

The fourth became my home
because it had no borders,

never asked its men
to take off their shirts.

I came from the western mountain.
I came from the black root.

I came from the bleeding leg
and the parted hair.

I came from the greasy hands,
from the embrace.

I came from the whispers in Spanish
and the broken rosary.

I came from the country air
and from the skull that faces me.

I came from the mound of wet dirt
and the left shoe.

I came from the right boot.
I came from the sweating hat.

I came from the railroad worker
and the masa cooker.

I came from the educated mother,
imitated the educated father.

I came from the dumb mother
and the dumb father.

I came from the psalm of the cottonwood
and the exploded tumbleweed,

from the shoeshine boy
and the tongue inside the black shoe.

I came from the braces of the handicapped
and from the broken rosary.

I came from the resemblance
and the bad blood.

I came from the good.
I came from the made-up story.

I came from the truth
and from the lie.

I came from the demon.
I came from the angel.

*

Enter my body.
The whole lesson lies inside the twig.

Enter my body.
The lesson in Spanish lies in the mind.

Enter my body.
The story can't be translated.

Enter my body.
God said it was okay to quit believing.

Enter my body.
I nestled in the chest of my wife and loved her.

Enter my body.
I never punished myself with a message from home.

Enter my body.
God said it only takes a groan and a prayer.

Enter my body.
I formed a language of rare clarity.

Enter my body.
God told me he would not miss me.

Enter my body.
I came back unsettled, uncombed.

Enter my body.
I could not look at what he taught me long ago—

How to bend at the knees,
darken my forehead with ashes,

shake in fear at surrounding shadows
that respond to faith, sin, and penance

entering my body with the rising cry
of those who quit believing

there are black shapes to show me
the exact spot to kiss on the dirt floor.

ROBERTO DENIES HE IS SUPERSTITIOUS

I don't believe in the scythe and sorrow,
can't pray to the long stick with carved faces on it.
I don't close my eyes to wait for the feather to brush my nose
and wake me with the knowledge of another world,
can't converse in silence with the second voice that
has two heads—one for the invisible father that breathes
on my neck, the second for the brother I never had.

I don't dream about that two-headed man,
won't convert to the glass of water and the broken flute.
I can't see the spirit draining out of the plant or
the tongue tasting the burned bread at the next altar
where my brothers and sisters are sacrificed
because they never told the truth.

I don't stare at paintings to watch them move,
have overlooked the velocity in the bullet,
turned my back on the flag and the torn fence.
I won't gather different kinds of roots,
crush them in my fists and rub the meat on my face.

I don't want to kneel and trace smoke from the cross
to outline my body like the soul
the vapors inhabit with their scent.
I can't believe in the beads of the revolution,
little balls of ivory tied together by a string,
rubbing my fingers over them to ward off
the shape that stands before me every time
I end my prayer with its name.

Roberto Talks to His Dead Brother

Esé, I know you didn't have time.
They tore you apart and your body flew
in the directions we pray to.

I was too young to care about
the flag that came back with you
and gathers dust in the trunk.

I don't know about your face.
I see it wherever I go, lie down
to dream my face is your face.

When you come back for me,
show me how far you flew before
this was the earth and that was childhood.

ROBERTO ANTICIPATES THESE GIFTS FROM HIS DYING FATHER

My father who owned
the town and gave orders,
the basket, the bread,
and the dripping flower
of the beloved.

The snorting bull
that survived the chase
through the streets,
the hoof and the eye,
the tail that was dipped in gold.

The hot food and
the safe milk that grew
out of my mother's rage,
the foot and the road
swept to greet the owl
before the old man's death.

Roberto Recalls His Dead Grandfather

He does not believe in the devil,
tells me the claw biting into my wrist
is the wrong nightmare to have.
He does not believe in God,
says the man above us is
a bird who flew too high,
trapped like a drunken angel
he believed in.

He does not care that I care,
says the old river of home
dried long ago, tells me
to quit believing in flowing water.
He has no reason to teach me
mutterings and grunts
of a secret circle,
shakes his head when
I invite him home
to tell me no one wants
to have dinner with someone
who quit eating long ago.

As he rises to leave he says,
"Write on white paper.
Always listen to the guitar.
Speak in English and hide
your Spanish to fool them
into thinking we are crazy
and have no tongue."

ROBERTO CONCERNING HIS YOUTH

I do not want to lie.
Not for truth.
Not for the visit to
the hormone tree
where I tried to tear
off the bark, chew it
and throw up my small voice.

I do not want to
enter the world with a kiss
or mistake the tree for the lust
of what I couldn't see.

Standing under
the branches,
I am finished.
It is not my ruin,
but the tree's.

ROBERTO GOES FOR A WALK AFTER THE WAR

The streets are quiet today.
Last night, they shot a kid for tagging these walls,
the bar owners claiming they were tired
of whitewashing the slogans.
I cross the street and think of the first letters
I scrawled when I learned to write,
early words I muttered in English
when I couldn't dream in Spanish anymore.

The streets are quiet tonight.
This evening, two boys crossed my path
and stared at me, their bright faces
falling into shadow so quickly,
I thought of the traitor standing
on the street corner reciting his poems,
daring me to turn him in.

The streets will be quiet tomorrow.
The guns and spray paint will be taken
to their neon graves, buried
as part of the dance where
empty arms of the boys carry
nothing but the shadows
their fathers passed to them
when they claimed them
as their sons.

Five Bird Songs

Somebody is breathing inside me—
Birds, the very earth.
—Shinkichi Takahashi

Fat Doves on the Back Fence

My wife says to come look.
One fat dove is sleeping on top of two others,
three bodies forming a bloated triangle.
The doves nestle into each other,
wait for the days when we used
to drop seed in the grass for them,
days of abundant heat when
the grains of hunger were the same seeds
that fell in our hair the year
we wandered in the trees,
lost but knowing we had
something to do with the pollen
that covered the earth.

Watching the Osprey at Point Reyes

We saw it dive and hook the fish,
flee the seagulls that tried to steal its catch.
The osprey landed on the pier like an angry pirate,
held onto the fish as if letting go
would mean another death.
One lone gull, perched a few feet away,
watched the hawk hold the fish,
but the osprey wouldn't eat
as the gull flapped around its head,
trying to take the fish out of its talons.

The osprey moved farther down the pier
as the gull stood where the meal landed.
The osprey pecked at the fish,
but wouldn't let go, as if letting go
meant the fish would come alive,
as if tearing too hard into the fish
would unleash a mark of flesh
against brown and white wings.

San Marcos Sparrows

Sparrows fight with each other,
zing over my head as if the horizon mattered
and elevation would sustain their wings.
Sparrows cry and chirp, but don't let go of me
as I sit and wait for the woman I love,
thinking about illness,
the decision to turn my back on things
that almost destroyed me.

Sparrows fight, then return to the fence
where they line up like reasons I had
for going the other way:
No more laughter.
Too few hands reaching out.
Too many voices wanting me.

Sparrows perch quietly on the fence
as the sun goes down in winter.
I will not bother these birds.
Their sudden movements rain down the fence,
dozens falling to the ground to peck in the dirt

so I can wish for more seeds,
regret what spilled at my feet,
sparrows springing back up the fence
when I stand to be blessed
with their noise, their droppings.

Trusting the Sparrow

Their brains scatter like smoke in your head
that burns when someone tells you what to do.
Their tiny wings spill shadows before you
like the last chance to blink your eyes.

The Zen master says the sparrow is
the most powerful creature on earth.
Volcanoes erupt sparrow wings over your face,
heat from their feathers a fire signaling
you are about to find a new world.

Feathers fall around your sanctuary,
your favorite park in the dizzy city.
Dozens of sparrows take over the grass,
clutching colors like the woman you love.

Gazing at these little birds finds you
flying toward the lake,
a feather nestled in your brain,
brushing against desire to disappear,
your sudden swoop toward the rising flock.

The Bird of Dreams

It was huge and hovered
with a blue and red head.

I couldn't see its wings,
thought of a giant hummingbird.

The bird came out of the gray sun
to trace lines on the face of a strange god

before flying into view,
suspended over me,

letting me know the sun
would turn back to yellow

upon the tapping bell,
the start of the music,

the moment I opened my eyes
to see the wing of color

was the extended arm I was shown
before I was born.

Everything was the apple and the glass of tea.
The mountain, the mold, the apron on the grandmother—
the neck of a brown baby holding its tiny head
to get rid of the black bees.
This is the end of a bad century,
the opening of a door that was never built into the chest.

A volume of loud wires coming out of the ground.
My grandfather rising from fifty-four years of death to see me.
The instrument carved out of bone.
A lock of hair from a famous seventeenth-century poet.
The disintegrating bible wishing it was another book.
A hanging arm sweeping the water out of the way.
My memory of flying through the tunnel that came out of
        nowhere.

A dog with wings and a cat with magic.
The sentiment and the sweat.
The blue chest of the working man and
the bare ankle of a young girl who drank beer.
The shadow of a young boy named Carlos and
the bare shoulders of a young girl who whispered.

The hunger of an older boy name José.
The hard work of a brother named Ramón with
a closeness and a disagreement among them.
A torn pair of work pants and
a stiff and muddy pair of gloves.
A pocket with two dollars crumbled inside.
A bare foot rubbing the bare back of a young girl.
The fourth can of beer.
The farmhouse that belonged to the family
and the chickens that were killed for food.
The cactus garden that killed two men when they fell in

and the pieces of green cactus that made them dream.
The green juice that started the earthquake,
the crushed flesh of cactus on their tongues
and its swelling that made them dream.
A garden hose washing away the blood.
The sparrow hovering over the trash can and
the back alley stinking of dog shit and drunken men.
Falling feathers interpreted for what they bring.

A church next door full of sermons and howling black faces.
The corner of the house where a young boy went to hide.
A single strand of hair found in a high school yearbook,
the forgotten idea that hiding it in there would lead to a
        different life.
The piano wounded by stones falling out of the cottonwood.
The willow tree spreading over the entire front yard
and the tiny white balls of gum that fell out of it one day.

The smell of shadows, trains, humor, tumbleweeds,
ice, empty parking lots, one or two torn knees,
a baseball glove, the first guy to cross the finish line,
the fear, the dread and the skill of escaping
so no one would start a list of smells.

Fear melted the memory of a lost boy.
The old house, the rosary around the neck,
the crushed dog in the road—
a sudden calling from behind to warn him
to come in and be still.
Who recalls how this ended when the men
built their ships and invaded to change the outcome?

The right to cry out and wait a whole century.
The embers, the lone piano, the oil lamps
damaged by a dream.
The ambition in the spine.
Who will insist on tapping the window to show
how easy it is to delay the next hundred years?

KNOWING

On this river
your sweat could
turn to freedom

the year could
become stories

the small town
the body's way
of knowing

On this river
a flood would
clean the soul

like a bad foot
embedded
in the mud

On this river
you could pray
like the mantis

hidden in
tall grass

the heart's way
of devouring
itself

from
Twilights and Chants
1987

SITTING

I sit alone at night.
The chest of my sleeping father
is the wind.
Someday small children
will come to call on me.

I sit alone in this room.
The flame of the candle
is the center of the spinning earth.
I know the moon will be full, again,
and make me want to ride away.

I sit alone by the window.
The shadows of the swinging branches are
jubilations from the family of trees.
I know which tree to sleep under
and awaken, entangled in the morning roots.

ONE DAY

I heard an owl call
in the middle of the day.
It was a surprise.
I had known the call
only at night.

I looked into
the tall cottonwoods,
but could not see the owl.
It kept hooting as
the sun blinded me.
The thick leaves kept
it hidden, but I could
hear it call.

I kept searching and
could not believe it.
An owl in the middle
of a hot day. Then,
there was a stillness.

I coughed and heard
the wind in the leaves.
Yes, the wind in
the shaking leaves.
That I could believe
because it did not
frighten me or
startle me away
from who I am.

THE OPINION AT POINT LOMA

Over the black balls of rock
comes the first idea,
shining silently to me.

Gliding over the thin branch of sky,
the wings of dirty seagulls,
then a boat following the bay line,
erased by whitecaps at the point.

I blow my nose in the wind
and remove my shoes.
No movement on the beach.
Even the moss on the cliffs hangs dry,
percolating a green odor,
an air floating in circles.

Finally, one person in the sand,
a large woman from where I sit,
bending, collecting colors
with her net.

My toes sink in the foam,
smearing mud to my knees.
A cold transparency,
light as membrane,
turns across my eyes,
beyond the beach.

The bare feet of the woman
slap closer to me.
In her net, shell gold flashes
and drips without a sound.

The idea lingers like a dying reef.
In thought, unsure.
Among the swallowing tides,
a new face mounts the shore.

A sea monster appears as a naked man,
the crab being poked at with a stick,
even the wet birds pecking for
a handout, ignoring my shouts.

In this moment,
in this long touch of knowing,
the wet body kisses its spirit,
gains the ugliness of the sandpiper,
the sheerness of the cliff
and the smell of the fish.

I dry myself on the rock
and recall the trembling
of the creature made love to
on the sand, a heart-deep cry
never heard again.

I wish for an idea to walk
along with on the shore,
the sudden feeling that
rivulets of water
leave marks on a man.

Now, in this long fog,
I sense light flashing somewhere
and I move up the beach
in half-sleep, knowing
I will miss the next boat.

That thought flows here and there,
washing in and out of the cove,
running with the force of
a crashing wave over black rocks,
like salt mesmerizing the air.

Traveling down the center
of something that is touching
the double vision of earth,
the edge of the desert that
separates the mind into
ways of seeing.

One path shows me
it is the same rainbow,
the black fortune of sky
that pulls the full moon high
over the eastern mountains,
its blinding ball turning
the sky purple as if that color

was better for the night
when the sun falls in the west
the instant the moon takes over,
the collision of spheres
a cross-eyed surprise.

The second sight is the way
of the sun that destroys
a lust for isolation inside
the canyons, demanding
the universe widen to allow
everything to align in sight,

all things to crash and form
this double field of circles,
their red expanse silhouetting
the cliffs in the western sky,
exposing them to the deep
bruises of eastern moon glow,

the miles of landscape caught
between the sun and moon,
the one moment of wanting to flee
the twilight century when
everything happens at once.

CHRISTMAS EVE, AGUIRRE SPRINGS, NEW MEXICO, 1984

1

If New Mexico is a myth, my return makes it real,
forces the sun to shine in winter and open
the mountain to me.

There is a gift of green below these towering cliffs
of the Organ Mountains.
Thousands of feet below, the desert floor
is the table where the ancient feast was held.

Up here, the secret forest is hidden inside
the canyons as the circle not taken or
destroyed by the desert sun that punishes
the living and preserves the dead.

Alone to face the immense cliffs on Christmas Eve,
the great fields of yucca that spread for miles,
a cold wind of a necessary December spent
recovering everything I can—miles of desert
and river and mountain I rage at.

2

High above me, the green peaks
are brushed with snow.
There is a waterfall up there,
miles from where I wait.

I do not attempt to reach it
or climb higher above the desert that
left me in the hidden growth of cottonwoods,

elms, and even mahogany—trees that
defend this high place with the need
to look upon the other side.

3

I can't see the birds
that cry in this forest.
Their sounds are different
from one another.

I know each note says
one thing and each
invisible soaring of wings
points in a new direction,
an unknown design of flight.

4

The cold kisses my fingers
as gray clouds pass over the peaks.
There is one gift waiting for me
across the stream that runs
down the mountain.

What I find here is
inside the ground,
already dissolved into
this high earth.
What remains is a trail
to the top, a cavity of rock
and cliff waiting for
the bright star to
shine in the sky.

Suddenly, I think about
the planets revolving beyond

our territory and I know
this place is the source of fire,
a wilderness spared
the evolution of planets
we are supposed to believe,

the sanctuary where the rocks
are the universe, canyon
and cliff galaxies of solid,
waiting space where my body
slams into rock and explodes
into constellations, uncharted
desert stars.

The nearest hills probe
themselves for men that run
through night canyons,
leaving footprints for
the sun in the morning.

Below concrete bridges
of the Rio Grande,
a Mexican father lurks
in the mud and searches
for his drowned son.

Somewhere on a street
in El Paso, under
a telephone pole
with no light,
a drunken couple scratch
each other's eyes out.

Many hours into sleep
and climbing long stairs,
I wake and step quickly
from childhood,
stare at the crucifix
growing blacker
on my bedroom wall.

Hiding the Stone Horse

for Barry Lopez

You found it in
the southern Arizona desert,
miles from nowhere,
yet so close to those
who would destroy it,
an eighteen-foot sculpture
the people carved
three hundred years ago.

It is the horse waiting
in the canyon,
catching its breath,
snorting as the morning light
revealed the illusion to you.

The wind and the heat
have rubbed its back
without witness.
Don't pinpoint its
location on a map.
Those of us who have
passed near know nothing
of the intaglio,

an abstraction that is there,
but not there, the black
horse galloping through
the centuries of rock
and sand to meet
the rough, brown hands
that carved it into life.

Absence of Lizards

I haven't seen a lizard
since I left the desert,
though I feel a lizard
behind my eyelids.
It darts in and out,
though I can't see it,
can't picture it jumping
off a rock to sit
inside my head.

I recall the invasion
of the white lizards,
the season they beat
the rain, overflowed
into the arroyos, sat
on the adobe walls
like cut-off fingers
twitching their tails,
waiting for my approach
before leaping into
the cactus like torn pieces
of paper I threw away,
white lizards flashing their
mocking dance at me.

The last giant lizard
I saw was shot by a kid
with a BB gun.
It was a foot long,
dark brown and fast.
The kid was a good shot,
left it in field across
from my house.

I found it on my walk,
ants crawling over the rocks
to get to it, hundreds
of them opening
the stiff, pregnant body
to get to the yellow eggs
spilling out of its belly
like kernels of corn
fertilizing the hot sand.

Testament

It was the red rosary in my grandmother's
trembling hands, my father and mother
leaving each other after thirty-two years,
the calendar photo of La Virgen de Guadalupe
tearing by itself inside the picture frame,
no one touching it the day of divorce,

my grandmother proclaiming it
a message from God saying we would suffer,
calling it a miracle when the picture
straightened itself inside the glass
without anyone touching it
the day after the family dissolved.

This is my belief in the adobe walls,
why I must touch the mud and
the blue sun deserves a legacy
for keeping legends from unraveling.

May we break out of the pueblo.
May we insist rosary beads do
explode into beads of sweat.
May we walk away from the house
like the sparrow swims through the worm
and the sea changes the shore
with its foam of blindness.

May we walk away like the mother
who has finished sewing the robe
for her mother's funeral.
May we finally walk away like the father
tired of waiting in his room to kiss
the weeping women that don't arrive.

SAVING THE CANDLES

She saves the ends of candles
after they have melted,
never throws them away,
keeps boxes full of melted candles.
She doesn't know how long she has to live,
five or ten years she says,
and tells me she wants to write
as much as she can before she goes on
to the next circle of light and silk,
like the one she describes in her poem
about the cocoon, butterfly,
and mulberry leaf.

We talk about the transformation of silk,
the last flame on the dying candle,
tears of wax petrified into
shapes of the heart.
Yet, I can't teach her about the smoke
after the candle goes out,
can't show her how the butterfly
comes out of the cocoon.

All I can do is find a new word
for courage without breaking the force
on that thread of silk and gather
candles I have in my house
so I can see what poetry has done,
envy how she found the image
begun by the worm in her tree,
and know the wax in her boxes of candles
waits for one more flame, one more
burning in the cycle of the mulberry leaf.

from
From the Restless Roots
1986

PRAYER

When we skip as wolves
over hot coals,
may the black earth divide
its fortunes among us.

When we drop cries
into watery canyons,
may our voices echo
as valuable gifts.

When we sleep in snow
to age our thoughts,
may we lose desire
to find the cause.

When we wake
as pilgrims,
may we claim everything
and walk alone.

SUNDAY

for Bill Broadwell

Sunday.
December.
Westside country road.
The pick-up slices through
the cold afternoon.

My friend, the insane truck driver,
hands me a bottle
and we enter the storm.

Rio Grande flowing
dead as icy glass.
Adobe walls slapped and fallen
before a warped telephone pole.

Frame of surplus Army bus
prehistoric green and for sale.
My beard refuses to grow
and we are already eighty-five
miles out of El Paso.

How Far Back?

As far back as the belly
of the river rises and falls,
flashes into summer lightning
and the frightening silence
of desert time.

As far back as clouds shake
above simple mountain peaks,
red and purple disturbances,
faces of rock closing their eyes.

As far back as the sunset deepens
against tomorrow's canyons,
abandons all wishes to smoke
the night with quiet rain.

As far back as my words take me,
as short a distance to my home,
the nest beneath the cottonwoods
twisting over the river
as far back as the earth goes.

ASCENDING

I listened to the melting snow,
my cold laughter.
I did not hear an echo.
I listened to the hush
of the canyon walls,
a weariness casting shadows
on the waiting rocks.

Then, I heard the blossoming,
the sigh, the answer.

"This is it," I whispered.
After all the snow, "This is it."

I waited and didn't know
what was there, except
the warmth of my body.
I leaned hard on the cliff walls
and rubbed my hands on the rock
to learn, at last, to know.

Four Towns, Don Juan de Onate Trail, New Mexico

La Union

The familiar dead dog at the side of the road,
a two-lane highway an explorer carved long ago.
Cottonfields, adobe and wood dwellings,
the new land always the old land.

A Mexican shovels a ditch in a field.
He looks at me with a toothless grin.
How many women and children depend
on him as he digs and the wind sweeps
his dirt over the migrant worker huts?

If I belonged here, I would help him dig,
knock at houses and ask for water
after a day in the fields.
The town ends below a grove of cottonwoods.

A sign over an empty shed says,
"Chile For Sale."
I stand in the smell of its harvest,
then follow the scattered trees.

Chamberino

In front of La Esperanza Bar, a worker sits
in back of a pickup, shakes it with drunken laughter.
He waves a can at me, yells the cantina is closed,
the beer truck is two days late.
This trail is a path of signs.
"Watch For Children."

Three boys dart across the highway.
A boy stands crying by his bicycle, loser of the fight.

I pause by the irrigation canal where
the overturned wagon spilled its cotton.
On the other side, a junkyard flashes in the sun,
marks my way through the sudden debris.

La Mesa

Cars that pass miss the deserted hacienda.
It hides behind a row of trees.
Years ago, a friend brought me here,
dreamed of buying it and becoming a recluse.

White arches retreat above the tumbleweeds.
In the courtyard, a rusted bell hangs over a well.
I try to ring it with the wire twisted beneath.
Silence pushes the vines up the walls.

If I had built these arches, I would not fear
the quiet cruelty I sense for miles.
A closed gas station is the center of town,
the end of it.

At last, I find a household.
Clothes on a line blow wet in the wind.
A woman stands in the door of her house,
waves me to the fields where her husband
drives a tractor to distant lines of barbed wire.

San Pedro

The last town is always the smallest, the one
where the explorer knew he could settle.
The church rises clear.
I avoid entering, tired of what I find inside.

Outside the church, two men sell grave
markers, statues of saints.
If I had a spot in the cemetery, I would lie
under the shadow of San Pedro, saint of travelers.

I step across the road to a fruit stand,
buy a bag of oranges from a small boy.
Crossing behind the church, a woman in black
approaches me as I drop peels to the ground.

She holds a dish of yellow seeds to me.
Silently, she tosses the seeds
at the green trees surrounding our heads.

Through the Creek, Cloride, New Mexico

At the turn in the canyon,
red sandstone walls reached
through clusters of cactus,
drumming water winding in low echoes,
the quietest tap of flowing motion,
the one toward which I moved
as I climbed upon smooth stones,
crawled below the green shadows
of pine and twisted cedar.

The color of the wilderness now blurred,
but I recall mountain blue jays
flashing across the stream,
vanishing into tiny wings of light.
Or, in my wake, fallen branches and logs split.
The moss on the rocks and the sun's blaze,
blinding water that far into the canyon,
breaking under thick cottonwoods,
huge leaves shaking in the wind.

My feet splashed in the creek,
sank over a carpet of pebbles that tore
into tiny mud clouds downstream.
This was when I penetrated the mountains
by walking in the water and light fell
off the walls, tiny lines cut in the sandstone,
a message carved by the wind,
lost and left up there,

above the canyon darkness,
the water running ahead of what
that message might spell.

DIAMONDBACK ON THE TRAIL

for Robert Burlingame

We were climbing
down the canyon
when the sudden head
and rattle moved in the sun.
We froze with respect
as it turned to us,
the enormous, poised body
revealing its claim
to the desert, its reason
for waking to leave us
suspended among
the cactus and red rocks.

We stepped back as you said
it was one of the biggest
you had ever seen,
your years in the canyons
flashing in memory like
the snake's quick tongue
flickering at the crossing
and the way we meet.
We stumbled upon
the slithering heart,
the cold, slow muscle
and the loud rattling,
its blood in beauty
one beat, its bone and body
a sudden grasp at the earth.

THE CLAY BOWLS

There are two of them
hidden behind each eye

in the mind, waiting
to be molded from wet

clay of the earth,
the river we drink from.

Listen to the echo
inside the great bowls.

It is deep water ringing,
drop by drop.

The clay reflects a clear surface,
a flash brimming to the top,

tears of water glistening
down their sweating stone hearts.

THE POEM AT THE END OF THE WORLD

Time fills it with the rushing madness
of travelers, your family.
They carry it to the edge,
their language for love.
Its words are written at your birth,
carved in the walls of growth,
of sheer explosion through the years
of casting about, alone.
Its lines are embedded among
the trains of migrating families,
figures nearing the end of their circle,
their breakup, their deaths.

The poem's images color themselves
into the future, visions of proud
mistakes and savage pronouncements
that tell you the distance to the last
word is not far.
The poem at the end of the world
has been fading for centuries,
then suddenly, glowing brightly,
falls into your path.

It is there, near the edge.
And, the poem at the end of the world
is not the last one you write,
but the first words to rise
as they create a new word for the sky.

ACKNOWLEDGMENTS

The author thanks the following journals where some of the new poems first appeared:

Beyond Words: "A Poem in Every Direction";

Bitter Oleander: "The Hiding," "Memorize," and parts of "The Burning";

Carnegie Mellon Review: "The Light at Mesilla";

Elixir: "Fever";

Hunger Magazine: parts of "The Burning";

New Letters: "Stopping Along the Rio Grande Near Hatch, New Mexico";

Portland Review: "The Walls";

Rio Grande Review: "Every Ten Years, a Hawk Kills Before Me";

Speakeasy: "Speak Easy";

TriQuarterly: "Hymn for the Tongue";

Verse: "Into" and "Immediacy";

Water-Stone: "My Brothers," "The Mask," and "The Promises of Glass";

Witness: "Rattlesnakes Hammered on the Wall."

About the Author

Ray Gonzalez is the author of nine books of poetry. His other titles from BOA include *The Hawk Temple at Tierra Grande* (2002), a winner of a 2003 Minnesota Book Award in Poetry, *Cabato Sentora* (1999); and *The Heat of Arrivals* (1996), a winner of a 1997 PEN/Josephine Miles Book Award. He is the author of two books of nonfiction: *Memory Fever* (1999), a memoir about growing up in the Southwest, and *The Underground Heart* (2002), which received the 2003 Carr P. Collins/ Texas Institute of Letters Award for Best Book of Nonfiction. He is also the author of two books of short stories: *The Ghost of John Wayne* (2001) and *Circling the Tortilla Dragon* (2002). His poetry has appeared in the 1999, 2000, and 2003 editions of *The Best American Poetry* and in *The Pushcart Prize: Best of the Small Presses 2000*. He is the editor of twelve anthologies, most recently *No Boundaries: Prose Poems by 24 American Poets*. He has served as Poetry Editor of *The Bloomsbury Review* for twenty-five years and founded *LUNA*, a poetry journal, in 1998. He received a Lifetime Achievement Award in Literature from the Border Regional Library Association in 2003 and is a Full Professor in the MFA Creative Writing Program at the University of Minnesota in Minneapolis.

BOA Editions, Ltd., American Poets Continuum Series

COLOPHON

Considerations of the Guitar: New and Selected Poems 1986–2005 by Ray Gonzalez was set in Caslon by Richard Foerster, York Beach, Maine. The cover design is by Steve Smock. Cover art, "The Unmoved" by Steve Carpenter, is courtesy of the artist. Manufacturing was by McNaughton & Gunn, Lithographers, Saline, Michigan.

The publication of this book was made possible, in part, by the special support of the following individuals:

Alan & Nancy Cameros
Gwen & Gary Conners
Bradley P. & Debra Kang Dean
Suzanne & Peter Durant
Dr. Henry & Beverly French
Dane & Judy Gordon
Kip & Deb Hale
Peter & Robin Hursh
Robert & Willy Hursh
Archie & Pat Kutz
Rosemary & Lewis Lloyd
Marianne & David Oliveiri
Boo Poulin
Deborah Ronnen
Paul & Andrea Rubery
Paul Tortorella
Pat & Michael Wilder
Glenn & Helen William